Awesome Addition and Super Subtraction

Developed and Published by
AIMS Education Foundation

This book contains materials developed by the AIMS Education Foundation. **AIMS** (**A**ctivities **I**ntegrating **M**athematics and **S**cience) began in 1981 with a grant from the National Science Foundation. The non-profit AIMS Education Foundation publishes hands-on instructional materials that build conceptual understanding. The foundation also sponsors a national program of professional development through which educators may gain expertise in teaching math and science.

Copyright © 2002, 2004, 2010 by the AIMS Education Foundation

All rights reserved. No part of this book or associated digital media may be reproduced or transmitted in any form or by any means—including photocopy, recording, or any information storage or retrieval systems—except as noted below.

New Copyright Policy!

A person purchasing this AIMS publication is hereby granted permission to make unlimited copies of any portion of it (or the files on the accompanying disc), provided these copies will be used only in his or her own classroom. Sharing the materials or making copies for additional classrooms or schools or for other individuals is a violation of AIMS copyright. Please visit www.aimsedu.org for further details.

AIMS Education Foundation
P.O. Box 8120, Fresno, CA 93747-8120 • 888.733.2467 • aimsedu.org

ISBN 978-1-60519-031-0

Printed in the United States of America

Table of Contents

Chinese Proverb 5
A Model of Mathematics and Operations 7

Building Conceptual Understanding 9
   Making Sense of Whole Number Operations 11
   Making Number/Operations Boards 13
   Place Value Labels 15
   Order, Please 17
   Middle Ground 19
   Building on Base 21
   Base Place: The Pluses 27
   Base Place: The Minuses 33
   Abacus Adventures 39
   Money Has Its Place 45

Meaningful Problem Solving 53
   Shape Frame Math 55
   Making Arrangements 63
   Math Spots 69
   Diving Into Diffies 87
   Diamond Diffies 89
   Digits in Disguise 93
   Clear the Deck 101
   Uncle Rebus Stories 103
   Sharing and Solving Stories 119

Playful and Intelligent Practice 121
   Cornering the Facts 123
   Saluting Subtraction and Addition 131
   Hands on the Addition and Subtraction Table 139
   Make It Even 141
   Roll Play 149
   Seek and Hide 151
   Spin to Win 155
   Fact Finding 159
   Tic Tac Ten and Twenty 161
   Rally With Differences 165
   Base Ten Bingo 169
   Who Has? Addition and Subtraction 181

I Hear and I Forget,

I See and I Remember,

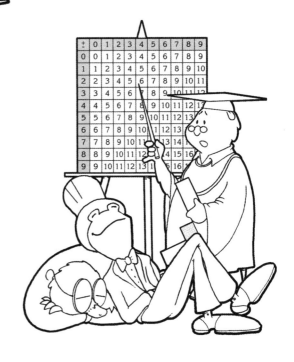

I Do and I Understand.
— Chinese Proverb

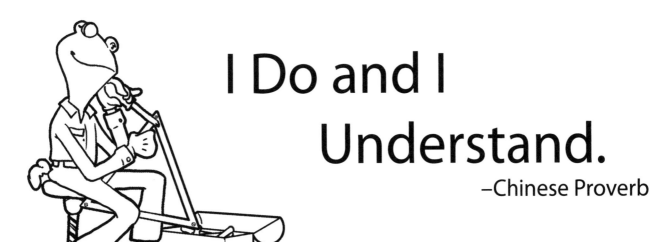

A Model of Mathematics and Operations

The learning experiences in *Awesome Addition and Super Subtraction* make use of the four learning environments embodied in the Model of Mathematics. The goal for students is to understand these two whole-number operations, and to this end students must be engaged in all four environments.

Doing
The circle represents hands-on experiences that include the use of manipulatives and models. Students will use manipulatives that help them internalize the meaning of addition and subtraction. It is of critical importance that students understand these operations at the concrete level.

Illustrating
The square symbolizes the picturing of information. It is often an important avenue for students to "picture" in the mind the meaning behind the operations. Students are given opportunity to interpret picture models of addition and subtraction as well as to draw their own.

Writing
The triangle represents addition and subtraction at an abstract level. It includes the use of symbols and numerals. The experiences in *Awesome Addition and Super Subtraction* make strong connections between the real-world circle experiences and the abstraction of the triangle. This connection will give insight into the meaning of addition and subtraction.

Thinking
The fourth learning environment is represented by the hexagon. The hexagon challenges students to reflect on the operations and to apply that knowledge to new learning situations.

The best learning experiences are those that make good use of all four environments. The use of this learning model will provide rich learning experiences.

Building Conceptual Understanding
Addition

Concrete/Manipulative Level
At this level, students join sets of objects in order to experience the basic operation in a concrete way.

Using countable objects
With *countable* objects, such as beans or buttons, the addition operation consists of joining two or more sets to form one set. Usually the sets have an unequal number of objects, but it is not a requirement. At the *manipulative* stage, students construct sets of countable objects, and then join or combine those sets into one. The move to combine the sets into one is referred to as the operation of addition. By counting, students can determine the number of objects in each set and also in the combined set—confirming that no objects have been added or lost in the transaction.

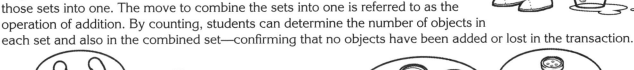

Using measured objects
Objects that have an attribute of length, such as Unifix cubes or straws, are appropriate for a *measured* model for addition. The addition of lengths consists of placing straws or Unifix cubes end to end so that one length is an extension of the other. Each length can be measured in units such as number of cubes or number of centimeters or inches.

   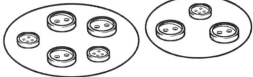

Representational/Pictorial Level
At the *representational* level, sometimes called the connecting stage, objects and actions are represented or depicted by pictures or diagrams. For addition, each set is pictured and arrows indicate that the sets have been combined into one.

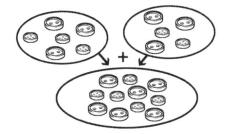   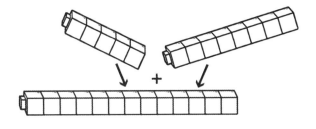

Counted model   Measured model

Abstract/Symbolic Level
At this level numerals, symbols, and relationship signs are used to represent the objects and actions of the concrete and representative levels. At the *symbolic* stage, objects can be counted and recorded symbolically with a plus (+) sign to represent the combination or union of sets. The equal (=) sign shows that no objects were gained or lost in the process. Thus the mathematical sentence 6 + 5 = 11 has meaning that can be reconstructed with manipulatives or translated in pictures. In the measured model, the plus (+) sign then represents the process of extending the length or building a train of Unifix cubes or straws.

Six and five is eleven.   Five plus eight equals thirteen.

6 + 5 = 11   5 + 8 = 13

Building Conceptual Understanding

Subtraction

Concrete/Manipulative Level
At this level, students separate a subset of objects from a larger set or compare two sets of objects, frequently unequal sets, in one-to-one correspondence.

Using countable objects
With countable objects, such as nuts and bolts, two kinds of experiences at the manipulative level may be explored—subtraction by separation or by comparison. In the separating model, students construct a set of objects, separate or "take away" some (occasionally all) of the objects, and count the remaining objects to determine the difference. In the comparison model, students match two sets of objects in one-to-one correspondence to determine relationships such as more than, less than, or equal to.

Using measurable objects
With objects that have a property that can be measured, such as length, the separating model consists of building a train of cubes or nuts and then breaking the train into two parts and removing or separating one part to determine the length of the remaining part. A comparison model similarly matches two trains of blocks in one-to-one correspondence to determine a relationship of more than, less than, or equal to.

Representational/Pictorial Level
At the representational level, sometimes called the connecting stage, objects and actions are represented or depicted by pictures or diagrams. For subtraction, a set is pictured and arrows indicate that a set has been separated into two parts or that two sets have been compared by matching elements in one-to-one correspondence.

Counted models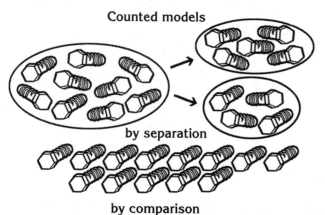

Measured models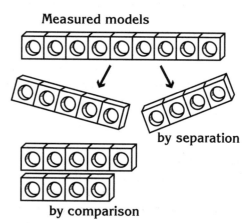

Abstract/Symbolic Level
At this level, numerals, symbols, and relationship signs are used to represent objects and actions of the concrete and representational levels. At the symbolic level, objects can be counted and recorded symbolically with a minus (−) sign to represent the separation of one set from another. The equal (=) sign shows that no objects were lost or gained in the process and that the sum of the parts equals the whole.

Nine objects take away five objects equals four objects

$$9 - 5 = 4$$

Nine objects compared to five objects:

Nine objects are four more than five objects. $9 > 5$ or $9 - 5 = 4$

Five objects are four less than nine. $5 < 9$ or $9 - 5 = 4$

Making Sense of Whole Number Operations

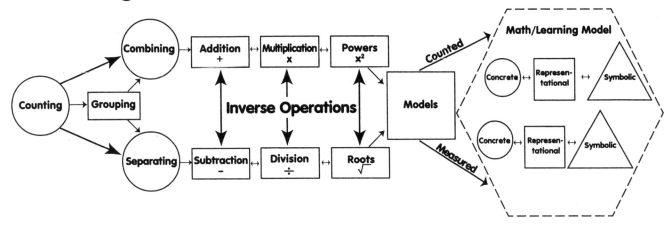

Levels of Operations

Concrete/Manipulative
Sets of objects are combined or separated and counted or measured in order to experience the basic operations in a concrete way.

Representational/Pictorial
Objects and actions are pictured and counted or measured.

Abstract/Symbolic
Numerals, symbols, and relationship signs are used to represent objects and actions at the concrete and representational levels.

Introduction

Traditionally the teaching of number concepts *begins* with introducing students to arithmetic through numerals and symbols. What elementary students need most is to make *meaning* of number and the basic operations through the use of concrete manipulatives and then make connections between the mathematics they study at the concrete level and the numerals and symbols at the abstract level. The difficulties that many children have with mathematics, specifically the potential for computational errors, are due in large part to their inability to make sense of the numeric symbols and the connection of any meaning to the algorithm.

The accompanying diagram speaks to us about a view of arithmetic that deals with groups. Students enter school and begin to learn to count by recognizing a one-to-one correspondence between an object and a number. Soon they recognize the number of objects in small groups without having to count each one. It is this recognition of groups that paves the way for considering each of the operations as one of combining or of separating groups of objects. Addition, multiplication, and raising to a power are all examples of a process of combining or joining while subtraction, division, and extracting a root are examples of a process of separating or partitioning. Each of the basic operations should be experienced at a variety of levels.

Beyond Understanding—The Basic Facts

A balanced mathematics program includes frequent doses of *playful, intelligent practice,* and *creative, real-world problem-solving* experiences that provide opportunity to apply the basic operations.

Making Number/Operation Boards

In much of the study of place value, students will need to use *Number/Operation Boards*. These are boards on which students can manipulate objects, group them, add and subtract, and connect values to the places numbers occupy.

Number/Operation Boards are constructed using the same pieces of construction paper. *Number Boards* will be on one side and *Operations Boards* will be on the other side.

1. To build a set of *Number/Operation Boards*, use 12" x 18" pieces of construction paper in yellow and blue and green.
   The yellow sheet will always be used for the ones place, the blue sheet will always be used for the tens place (numbers to 99), and the green will always be used for the hundreds place (numbers to 999).
2. You will need to prepare one set of boards per student.
3. One side of each paper will be left blank. This is the *Number Board* side. The *Number Boards* will be used to teach the grouping of objects into sets of tens and hundreds.
4. On the other side of the paper, draw lines with a black marker to divide the paper into thirds along the 18" dimension. Add strips of pink paper to the bottom third of each paper to show the division of part-part-whole.
5. Laminate these sheets of construction paper for durablity.
6. *Place Value Labels* can be added.

Number Boards (side one)

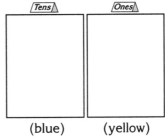

Number Boards with labels: tens and ones

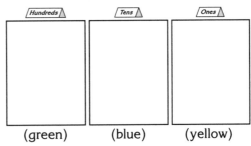

Number Boards with labels: hundreds, tens, and ones

Operation Boards (side two)

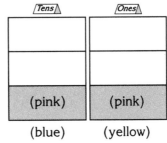

Operation Boards with labels: tens and ones

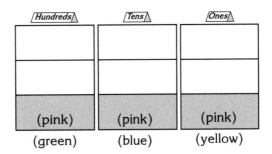

Operation Boards with labels: hundreds, tens, and ones

Place Value Labels

Hundreds	Tens	Ones
Hundreds	Tens	Ones
Hundreds	Tens	Ones

Order, Please

Purpose of the Game
Students will make all possible three-digit numbers with each roll and correctly order them.

Materials
Three dice
Pencils
Scratch paper

Management
1. This game can be played with two to four players.

Directions
1. Roll all three dice.
2. Using the numbers rolled, make as many three-digit numbers as possible.
3. Record each three-digit number and arrange them from smallest to largest on the scratch paper.
4. One point is received for each different number.
5. Play continues until a set time has passed. The player with the most points is the winner.

Variation
Add additional dice until the one millions place is reached (seven dice).

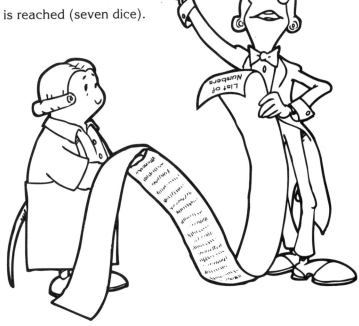

Purpose of the Game
Students will build two three-digit numbers with as large a range as possible.

Materials
Playing cards (see *Management 2*)
Scratch paper
Pencil

Management
1. This is a two-player game.
2. Each pair of students needs the one (ace) through nine in all four suits from a deck of cards.

Directions
1. Shuffle the cards and deal six cards to each player.
2. Use the six cards to create two three-digit numbers with as large a range as possible. Lay the cards face up on the table to show the numbers created.
3. When all numbers are created, turn over the top three cards from the stack to make a new number. The first card turned over is the number in the hundreds place. The second card turned over is the number in the tens place. The third card turned over is the number in the ones place.
4. If the new number falls between a player's two three-digit numbers, a point is scored. For example, with the cards 5, 2, 1, 4, 9, and 6, a player might create the numbers 469 and 521. If the three cards turned over make the number 634, a point would not be received because the number falls outside of the cards' range. If the numbers created had been 124 and 965, a point would have been received.
5. Play continues until one player has a specific number of points or until time runs out. (10 points or 10 minutes)

Variation
Start with additional cards and make four- and five-digit numbers.

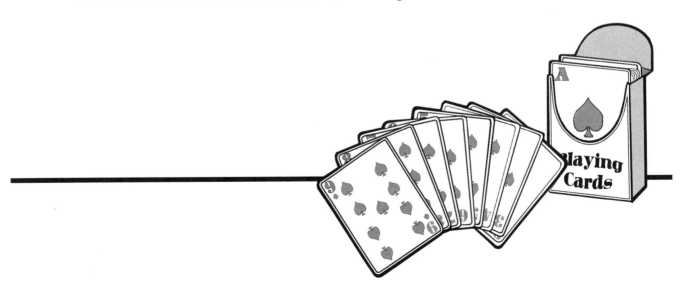

AWESOME ADDITION AND SUPER SUBTRACTION

Building on Base

Topic
Place value

Key Question
What is the value of your building?

Learning Goals
Students will
- construct buildings or designs using Base Ten Blocks, and
- calculate the value of each building or design.

Guiding Document
*NCTM Standards 2000**
- *Count with understanding and recognize "how many" in sets of objects*
- *Use multiple models to develop initial understandings of place value and the base-ten number system*
- *Connect number words and numerals to the quantities they represent, using various physical models and representations*
- *Understand the effects of adding and subtracting whole numbers*

Math
Number sense
  place value

Integrated Processes
Observing
Classifying
Comparing and contrasting

Materials
Place Value Labels (see *Management 3*)
Number Boards (see *Management 4*)
Base Ten Blocks
Student page

Background Information
Students need time to explore the Base Ten Blocks. This activity provides an opportunity to construct "buildings" or designs and then asks the students to find the value of what they built.

The Base Ten Blocks used in this activity show a proportional relationship. The longs are ten times larger than the units, and the flats are ten times larger than the longs. Ones are clearly smaller and the hundreds are clearly larger. These blocks reflect a clear relationship for ones, tens, and hundreds. The units, representations of ones, can be grouped to make a long. The longs, representations of tens, can be exchanged for flats. These experiences help the students develop a sense of the value of each place and each piece.

The grouping and exchanging that takes place with the Base Ten Blocks provide opportunity for the students to develop an understanding of the value of the place as well as the value of the face of the digits. A collection of three longs and four units would be displayed as three tens and four ones and would have a face value of 34.

Management
1. It is assumed that the students have had prior grouping experiences in which the idea of each place holding only nine units or sets has been developed.
2. The focus is on exploration of the materials.
3. Duplicate one set of *Place Value Labels* for each student group or make your own using folded index cards.
4. Each pair of students will need ones, tens, and hundreds (yellow, blue, and green) *Number Boards*.
5. Base Ten Blocks are available from AIMS (item number 4008).

Procedure
1. Distribute a set of Base Ten Blocks to each group of students.
2. Ask the students to open the box of materials and remove one block of each size.
3. Challenge the students to find the value of each of the pieces if the unit is equal to one. (The students should discover and describe that the long is equal to ten and the flat is equal to 100.) Direct a discussion in how the students arrived at the value of each of the pieces.

4. Direct the students to create a design or building with the Base Ten Blocks.
5. Distribute the *Number Boards* and *Place Value Labels* to each group and show them how to set up the boards with the ones (yellow) on the right, the tens (blue) in the center, and the hundreds (green) on the left.
6. Tell students that they will be decomposing (disassembling) their designs/buildings in order to find their values. Explain that the students will be placing the units, longs, and flats on the appropriate the *Number Boards*. (Color, position, and label indicate the value of each place. The Base Ten Blocks are being used in this activity as single objects in their placement. The unit on the ones board represents **one** unit, the long on the tens board represents **one** ten, and the flat on the hundreds board represents **one** hundred. The board represents the value while the Base Ten Blocks serve only to reinforce the placement.)
7. Remind students that only nine of each piece can be on any one board. Tell them that if it is necessary, they can trade units for longs and longs for flats.
8. Have the students share the values of their buildings or designs.
9. Distribute the student page. Have students work through the problems.

Connecting Learning
1. Why do you think the units, longs, and flats have different values?
2. Why was it important to discover the value of the pieces?
3. What would the value of 10 flats be?
4. What limited the size of the building or design?
5. How big would a design or building be that had a value of six? What about a value of 600?
6. What did you learn by doing this activity?

* Reprinted with permission from *Principles and Standards for School Mathematics,* 2000 by the National Council of Teachers of Mathematics. All rights reserved.

Building on Base

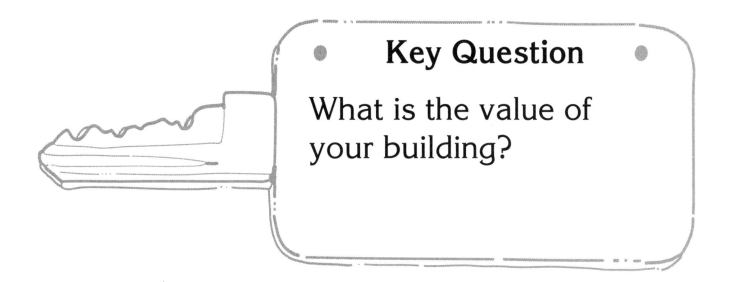

Key Question

What is the value of your building?

Learning Goals

Students will:

- construct buildings or designs using Base Ten Blocks, and

- calculate the value of each building or design.

Building on Base

1. What is the value of your building?

   _____
   Value

2. Design a building using three flats, seven longs, and two units.

Flats	Longs	Units

   What is its value?

   _____
   Value

3. What is the value of a building that has two flats, five longs, and 14 units?

Flats	Longs	Units
   Before trading

Flats	Longs	Units
   After trading

   _____
   Value

4. Design a building that uses more than nine longs. Have a partner determine its value. Remind your partner that he or she may have to do some trading.

   What did you determine the value of your building to be?

   _____
   Value

   What did your partner determine its value to be?

   _____
   Value

   } Explain any difference on the back of this paper.

AWESOME ADDITION AND SUPER SUBTRACTION

Building on Base

Connecting Learning

1. Why do you think the units, longs, and flats have different values?

2. Why was it important to discover the value of the pieces?

3. What would the value of ten flats be?

4. What limited the size of the building or design?

5. How big would a design or building be that had a value of six? What about a value of 600?

6. What did you learn by doing this activity?

Topic
Addition

Key Question
How can we use *Operation Boards* to help us solve addition problems?

Learning Goals
Students will:
- construct manipulative models to represent operations of addition, using one-, two-, and three-digit numbers; and
- solve two- and three-digit addition problems with and without regrouping.

Guiding Document
NCTM Standards 2000*
- *Count with understanding and recognize "how many" in sets of objects*
- *Use multiple models to develop initial understandings of place value and the base-ten number system*
- *Connect number words and numerals to the quantities they represent, using various physical models and representations*
- *Understand the effects of adding and subtracting whole numbers*

Math
Number sense
   place value
Number and operations
   addition
Expanded notation

Integrated Processes
Observing
Classifying
Comparing and contrasting

Materials
Place Value Labels (see *Management 3*)
Operation Boards (see *Management 4*)
Base Ten Blocks
Yellow, green, blue, and pink sticky notes, 3" x 3" (see *Management 5*)

Background Information
The Base Ten Blocks used in this series of activities show a proportional relationship. The longs are ten times larger than the units, and the flats are ten times larger than the longs. These blocks reflect a clear relationship for ones, tens, and hundreds. The units (the ones) can be grouped to make a long. The longs can be exchanged for flats. These experiences help the students develop a sense of the value of each place. Ones are clearly smaller and the hundreds are clearly larger.

The grouping and exchanging that take place with the base ten materials provides opportunity for the students to develop an understanding of the value of the place as well as the face value of the digits. A collection of three longs and four units would be displayed as 3 tens and 4 ones and would have a face value of 34.

The sticky notes used to record the numbers on the *Operation Boards* will provide for an opportunity to informally explore expanded notion.

Management
1. It is assumed that the students have had prior grouping experiences in which the idea of each place holding only nine blocks or sets has been developed.
2. This activity should be spread out over several days.
3. Copy the *Place Value Labels* on card stock or make your own from folded index cards. Each pair of students needs one set.
4. Each pair of students will need ones, tens, and hundreds (yellow, blue, and green) *Operation Boards*. The *Operation* side of the board is the one divided into three sections.
5. The sticky notes will be used to record the addition problems. The colors should match the colors of the *Operation Boards*.
6. Base Ten Blocks are available from AIMS (item number 4008).

Procedure
Part One—Addition Without Regrouping
1. Pair students and give each pair ones, tens and hundreds *Operation Boards* and a set of *Place Value Labels*. Distribute one set of Base Ten Blocks for every two pairs of students.
2. Direct students to position the boards with the pink section at the bottom. Explain that the yellow represents the ones place, the blue represents the tens place, and the green represents the hundreds place. Ask them to place *ones, tens, and hundreds* labels above the appropriate boards. (Color, position, and

label indicate the value of each place. The Base Ten Blocks, although proportional in their value and used in that manner in *Building on Base*, are being used in this activity as single objects in their placement. The unit on the ones board represents **one** unit, the long on the tens board represents **one** ten, and the flat on the hundreds board represents **one** hundred. The board represents the value while the Base Ten Blocks serve only to reinforce the placement.)

3. Present a number problem for the class to solve. Example: There are 17 boys and 12 girls in the class. How many students are in the class altogether?
4. Direct the students to place longs and units in the top sections of their *Operation Boards* to represent the number of boys in the class. Ask them to name the number in terms of tens and ones. [1 ten and 7 ones]
5. Tell them to place longs and units in the middle sections of their *Operation Boards* to represent the number of girls in the class. Ask them to name the number in terms of tens and ones. [1 ten and 2 ones]
6. To find the solution to the question "How many students are in the class altogether?" have the students combine the longs and units from the top two sections into the pink bottom sections of the *Operation Boards*. Ask them to name the number in terms of tens and ones. [2 tens and 9 ones] Have them name the number as a total. [29 students altogether]
7. On the board, record the number sentence as 17 + 12 = 29. Explain that this + sign tells them to combine all the longs and units.
8. Continue presenting number problems in this manner, being careful not to require the students to regroup at this time. Add number problems that require the use of the flats (hundreds) if your students are ready for them.

Part Two—Addition With Regrouping
1. Direct students to position their *Operation Boards* with the pink sections at the bottom.
2. Write "9" on the board. Tell the students to build this number on the top section of the ones (yellow) *Operation Board*. Check to make sure the students have placed the units on the appropriate section and board.
3. Direct the students to place their tens place (blue) *Operation Boards* next to and to the left of their yellow boards.
4. Write "+7" on the board and tell them to place seven units in the middle section of their yellow boards. Check to make sure the students placed the units on the appropriate section and board.
5. Present a number sentence such as: There were nine children playing soccer. Seven more children joined them. How many children were there altogether?
6. Have the students build the solution to this number sentence on their boards. Pause, waiting for someone in the group to possibly determine that they have a set of ten ones. Ask them what they think they should do with the set of ten. [Trade it in for a long and move the long over to the tens (blue) board.] If they do not think of this on their own, direct them to make this move. Have them move their units to represent the sum or total to the bottom pink sections of their boards. Check to make sure the students have placed one long and six units in the appropriate places on their boards. Ask the students to name the number that represents the solution to the question. [16 children playing soccer or one ten and six ones]
7. Continue presenting additional number problems that require the students to regroup. Use higher numbers such as 28 + 36, 116 + 35, and 236 + 127.

Part Three—Addition Without Regrouping, Recorded
1. Explain that students will be using the same type of board they have been using, but now they will include sticky notes to record the numbers they have built. Give each student sticky notes in all four colors.
2. Using longs and units, direct the students to build the number 37 on their boards. Ask the students to name the number of tens represented. [3] ...ones. [7]

3. Ask the students to place sticky notes on these boards, matching colors of sticky notes to colors of boards. Tell them to record the number 7 on their yellow sticky notes and a 30 on their blue sticky notes. Discuss how these numbers represent the number of ones and sets of tens located on their boards.
4. In the middle section of the boards, have the students build the number 31. Ask the students to name the number of tens and ones represented. Direct them to write 30 and 1 on the appropriate sticky notes.
5. Present a number story such as: On Monday, there were 37 tickets sold for a concert. On Tuesday, 31 more tickets were sold. How many tickets were sold altogether?
6. Direct the students to build the solution to the question on their boards. Check for appropriate grouping in the tens and ones places on the boards. Ask the students to name and record the solution to the question on the sticky notes. [60 and 8]
7. Tell the students to remove the sticky notes and stack them on each other and sequence them as an addition problem. Have them record the solution on a pink sticky note.

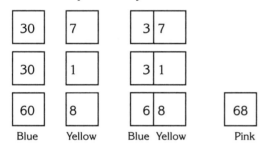

8. Ask the students to read the numbers as in the number sentence. [37 + 31 = 68]
9. Direct the students to add a plus sign and an equal sign to the problem.

Part Four—Addition With Regrouping, Recorded
1. Using the *Operation Boards* and sticky notes, tell the students to build and record 129 in the top sections and 163 in the middle sections of their boards.
2. Present a number problem such as: In the morning, there were 129 students present at the soccer clinic. In the afternoon, 163 more students joined the clinic. How many students attended the clinic altogether?
3. Give the students a pink sticky note on which to record the + sign. Have them place the plus sign to the left of the *Operation Boards*.
4. Tell them to combine the units in the ones place and to move them to the pink portion of the board. Ask them to name the number of ones. Point out that they have a set of ten and that they will need to trade these for a long.

5. Direct them to bring the long up to the top portion of the tens place and to record a small one above the two on the sticky note to show that they have added a set of ten. Tell them the small one is a way of reminding them that they have regrouped the ones into a set of ten. Instruct them to name and record the number of ones in the ones box at the bottom of their boards.
6. Have the students bring all the sets of ten down to the lower part of the board. Tell them to name and record the total number of sets of ten on a pink sticky note at the bottom. Direct them to do the same with the flats in the hundreds place.
7. Direct the students to remove the sticky notes and to line them up at the bottom of the boards. Ask the students to name the number written in the bottom recording boxes. [292]

8. Repeat this procedure with several other number combinations that require regrouping.

Connecting Learning
1. How did you decide how many objects to put in each section of your boards?
2. What do you need to do when you have more than nine units in the ones place?
3. What does the symbol + tell you to do?
4. Build a number story on your board and then write the number story using numerals. Tell your story to the class.
5. How did the *Operation Boards* help you solve addition problems?

* Reprinted with permission from *Principles and Standards for School Mathematics*, 2000 by the National Council of Teachers of Mathematics. All rights reserved.

Key Question

How can we use *Operation Boards* to help us solve addition problems?

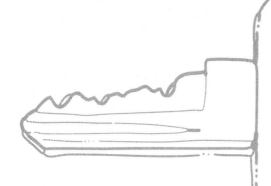

Learning Goals

Students will:

- construct manipulative models to represent operations of addition, using one-, two-, and three-digit numbers; and

- solve two- and three-digit addition problems with and without regrouping.

Connecting Learning

1. How did you decide how many objects to put in each section of your boards?

2. What do you need to do when you have more than nine units in the ones place?

3. What does the symbol + tell you to do?

4. Build a number story on your board and then write the number story using numerals. Tell your story to the class.

5. How did the *Operation Boards* help you solve addition problems?

Base Place — THE MINUSES

Topic
Subtraction

Key Question
How can we use *Operation Boards* to help us solve subtraction problems?

Learning Goals
Students will:
- construct manipulative models to represent operations of subtraction, using one-, two-, and three-digit numbers; and
- model and solve subtraction story problems with and without regrouping.

Guiding Document
NCTM Standards 2000*
- *Count with understanding and recognize "how many" in sets of objects*
- *Use multiple models to develop initial understandings of place value and the base-ten number system*
- *Connect number words and numerals to the quantities they represent, using various physical models and representations*
- *Understand the effects of adding and subtracting whole numbers*

Math
Number sense
   place value
Number and operations
   subtraction
Expanded notation

Integrated Processes
Observing
Classifying
Comparing and contrasting

Materials
Place Value Labels (see *Management 3*)
Operation Boards (see *Management 4*)
Base Ten Blocks
Student page

Background Information
The Base Ten Blocks used in this series of activities show a proportional relationship. The longs are ten times larger than the units, and the flats are tens times larger than the longs. These blocks reflect a clear relationship for ones, tens, and hundreds. The units (the ones) can be grouped to make a long. The longs can be exchanged for flats. These experiences help the students develop a sense of the value of each place. Ones are clearly smaller and the hundreds are clearly larger.

The grouping and exchanging that take place with the base ten materials provide opportunity for the students to develop an understanding of the value of the place as well as the face value of the digits. A collection of three longs and four units would be displayed as 3 tens and 4 ones and would have a face value of 34.

The recording sheet reinforces the concept of place value and subtraction. It also more closely matches the traditional algorithm while connecting it to a model.

Management
1. It is assumed that the students have had prior grouping experiences in which the idea of each place holding only nine blocks or sets has been developed.
2. This activity should be spread out over several weeks.
3. Copy the *Place Value Labels* on card stock or make your own using folded index cards. Each pair of students needs one set.
4. Each pair of students will need the ones and tens (yellow and blue) *Operation Boards*. The *Operation* side of the board is the one divided into thirds.
5. Make sure the students are solving problems that relate to stories. It is of little value to simply add or subtract numbers.
6. The student page is designed to help the students keep the digits in the correct columns as well as offer them a written record of what they are manipulating on the *Operation Boards*.
7. Base Ten Blocks are available from AIMS (item number 4008).

Procedure
Part One—Subtraction Without Regrouping
1. Pair students and give each pair ones and tens *Operation Boards* and a set of *Place Value Labels*. Distribute one set of Base Ten Blocks for every two pairs of students.
2. Direct students to position the boards with the pink sections at the top. Remind them that the yellow

AWESOME ADDITION AND SUPER SUBTRACTION

represents the ones place and the blue represents the tens place. Ask them to place *ones* and *tens* labels above the appropriate boards. (Color, position and label indicate the value of each place. The Base Ten Blocks, although proportional in their value and used in that manner in *Building on Base*, are being used in this activity as single objects in their placement. The unit on the ones board represents **one** unit, the long on the tens board represents **one** ten, and the flat on the hundreds board represents **one** hundred. The board represents the value while the Base Ten Blocks serve only to reinforce the placement.)

2. Present a number problem for the class to solve such as: Nick had 15 action figures. He gave his brother Andrew 3 of them. How many did Nick have left?
3. Direct the students to place longs and units in the top pink sections of their *Operation Boards* to represent the number of action figures Nick had. Write 15 on the board and then write – 3 below it. Ask the students what the minus sign represents in this story. [The fact that Nick is giving away something.]
4. Tell the students to move three units from the 15 into the middle section of the yellow board. Discuss what this number of units represents. [These units represent the action figures Nick has given away.] Tell students to move the longs and units that are left in the top pink sections all the way down to the bottom sections.
5. Repeat this with two- and three-digit problems until the students have developed a sense of whole-part-part for subtraction. Be sure to select numbers that do not require regrouping.
6. Discuss with the students how subtraction and addition are related. Direct them to turn the boards around to check a subtraction problem. If their sum matches the original number they began with in their subtraction problem, they can assume their subtraction answer is correct.

Part Two—Subtraction With Regrouping
1. Present the following problem to the students: Charlie scored 23 points in a basketball game. Mary scored 9 points. How many more points did Charlie score? Write the number sentence on the board 23 – 9 = ?
2. Ask the students what they will need to place in the pink section of their *Operation Boards* to represent 23. Make sure the students place two longs on the blue board and three units on the yellow board.
3. Ask the students to take away nine units from the ones section to represent the number of points Mary scored. Pause and wait while the students determine how to remove the nine units. Ask them how they think they can solve the problem. Guide them in trading one of the longs for ten units. Place the ten units with the three original units. The students will then be able to move nine units into the middle section of the board.
4. Work the problem on the board by crossing out the two in the tens place and adding a one above the two in the tens place. Add a small ten above the three indicating 13 in the ones place. Discuss how there are now 13 units temporarily in the ones place.
5. Continue working with additional problems that require regrouping using two- and three-digit problems.

Part Three—Recording Subtraction With and Without Regrouping
1. Distribute the student page to each student. Select a problem for the students to solve.
2. Direct the students to solve the problem on the *Operation Boards* as they also record the problem and solve it on the student page. Point out that they will need to place the digits for the problem in the correct place on the student page.

Connecting Learning
1. How did you decide how many objects to put in each section of your boards?
2. What do you need to do when you have more than nine units in the ones place?
3. What does the symbol – tell you to do?
4. Build a number story on your board and then write the number story using numerals. Tell your story to the class.
5. How did the *Operation Boards* help you solve subtraction problems? How did the student page help you in solving the problems?

* Reprinted with permission from *Principles and Standards for School Mathematics*, 2000 by the National Council of Teachers of Mathematics. All rights reserved.

Key Question

How can we use *Operation Boards* to help us solve subtraction problems?

Learning Goals

Students will:

- construct manipulative models to represent operations of subtraction, using one-, two-, and three-digit numbers; and

- model and solve subtraction story problems with and without regrouping.

Operation Boards

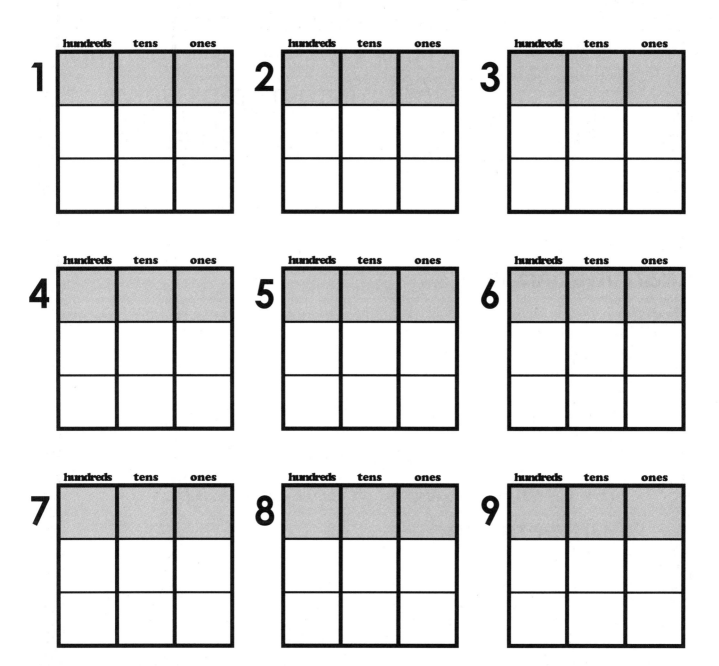

Connecting Learning

1. How did you decide how many objects to put in each section of your boards?

2. What do you need to do when you have more than nine units in the ones place?

3. What does the symbol – tell you to do?

4. Build a number story on your board and then write the number story using numerals. Tell your story to the class.

5. How did the *Operation Boards* help you solve subtraction problems? How did the student page help you in solving the problems?

Topic
Number sense

Key Question
How can we use an abacus to build, write, and read numbers?

Learning Goals
Students will:
- construct a model abacus; and
- build, write, and read numbers using the model.

Guiding Document
NCTM Standards 2000*
- *Use multiple models to develop initial understandings of place value and the base-ten number system*
- *Develop a sense of whole numbers and represent and use them in flexible ways, including relating, composing, and decomposing numbers*
- *Connect number words and numerals to the quantities they represent, using various physical models and representations*

Math
Counting
Number sense
   place value

Integrated Processes
Observing
Classifying
Comparing and contrasting
Applying

Materials
For each student:
   one graham cracker
   three large gumdrops
   three coffee stirrers
   small cup of circular cereal
   frosting (see *Management 2*)
   one craft stick
   student recording page

For the class:
   The Warlord's Beads
      (see *Curriculum Correlation*)
   scissors

Background Information
The progression of place value lessons usually begins with students using a groupable manipulative, such as beans and bean sticks; sticks and bundles; or Unifix cubes and trains representing ones, tens, and hundreds. On the abacus, the position of the numbers is what gives the numbers their values; therefore, it creates a bridge from the concrete groupable manipulative experiences to the abstract use of written numbers.

In this activity, the students will be using an abacus to build, write, and read whole numbers. The abacus provides a visual representation and hands-on experience. The operator of the abacus performs mental calculations as he or she determines the place value and face value of the digits.

There are several types of abaci. The type of abacus that the students will be using in this activity consists of a series of vertical sticks that will represent the ones, tens, and hundreds places. The right-most stick on the abacus is the ones place, the next stick to the left is the tens place, the next to the left is the hundreds place, and so on. The students will use circular cereal on these sticks to represent the digits of the numbers they will be asked to build, write, and read.

Management
1. This activity should follow concrete experiences with the children building numbers using other manipulatives such as Unifix cubes and Base Ten Blocks. This activity will serve as a transition, helping to form a bridge from the concrete blocks to the abstract numbers on a page.
2. Each student will need a small amount of frosting that will be used as an adhesive to attach the gumdrops to the graham cracker.
3. To prevent the graham crackers from breaking, place the coffee stirrers into the gumdrops before attaching the gumdrops to the graham crackers.
4. The number of stirrers and gumdrops will depend on your place value focus. Each student will need one gumdrop and one stirrer per place. Two of each would be needed to work with the ones and tens places, three of each would be needed to work through the hundreds place, etc.
5. Relate the work that the students will be doing on the abacus to their prior experiences with groupable manipulatives.

6. Building numbers such as 301 on the abacus will help students to recognize the need for a zero in the middle to represent the empty space and will help them to see that it should not be written 3001 because that would place the 3 in the thousands place.

Procedure

1. Read the book *The Warlord's Beads*.
2. Tell the students that they will be constructing an abacus similar to the one that Chaun created. Explain that an abacus is a tool they will use for counting, building, reading, and writing numbers.
3. Give each student the following items: one graham cracker, a small cup of circular cereal, a small amount of frosting, two or three gumdrops, and two or three coffee stirrers.
4. Tell your students to insert one coffee stirrer into the top of each gumdrop.
5. Direct the students to use a small amount of frosting to attach the gumdrops to the graham crackers so that they are as centered and evenly spaced as possible.
6. Instruct your students to put nine cereal pieces on each coffee stirrer. Cut students' stirrers just above the last cereal piece so that each place can hold only nine pieces. This will reinforce the concept of trading up.
7. Tell your students to remove all cereal pieces from their abaci.
8. Ask the students to put their fingers on the ones place and check for understanding. Do the same for the tens and hundreds places, if appropriate for your students.
9. When you have established that the students can recognize each place and its value, you can begin to build numbers. Place five circular cereal pieces in the ones place on your abacus. Tell your students to do the same. Ask them to read the number out loud. [five ones] Write the number on the board. Ask the students to clear their abaci. Tell them to build the number 8 on their abaci. Ask them to read the number out loud. [eight ones] Check for accuracy and write the number 8 on the board. Have them clear their abaci.
10. Build the number 23 on your abacus and instruct the students to read the number. Have the students build 23 on their abaci. Question them about the number 23. What digit is in the tens place? What is its value? What digit is in the ones place? What is its value? Continue using the abacus to build and read numbers through the hundreds or thousands place as appropriate.
11. Instruct your students to add three cereal pieces to the ones place. Have them identify the new number. [26]
12. When the students demonstrate an understanding of the process used to build numbers on the abacus, allow them several opportunities to also write the numbers they are building and reading. (A student recording page is provided for this purpose.) By writing the number displayed on the abacus, they are connecting the objects in each place to the number that represents those objects.

Connecting Learning

1. If Chaun were holding up two toes and three fingers, how many boxes would his father have counted? [230]
2. What is the value of five in the ones place? [5]
3. What is the value of three in the tens place? [30]
4. What is the largest number you could make with three stirrers and six pieces of cereal?
5. How does an abacus work?

Extensions

1. When your students have become proficient with the building, writing, and reading of numbers, and are able to tell the place value and face value of each digit, complete some of the exercises described on the *Abacus Extensions* page.
2. Have students add a fourth gumdrop to their abaci and practice building numbers in the thousands.

Curriculum Correlation

Pilegard, Virginia Walton. *The Warlord's Beads*. Pelican Publishing Company. Gretna, Louisiana. 2001.

* Reprinted with permission from *Principles and Standards for School Mathematics,* 2000 by the National Council of Teachers of Mathematics. All rights reserved.

Key Question

How can we use an abacus to build, write, and read numbers?

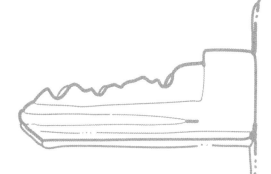

Learning Goals

Students will:

- construct a model abacus; and

- build, write, and read numbers using the model.

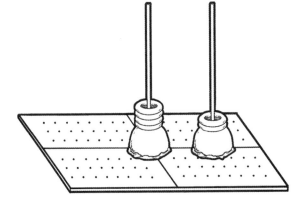

Extensions

Focus on Computation
- Add and subtract using the abacus. For example, have the students build the number 23. Ask them to add seven pieces of cereal. Discuss the trading that takes place.

Focus on Place Value
- Add large numbers to the abacus. For example, have students build the number 12 and then add 25. Discuss how you don't add 25 pieces of cereal, you put two pieces in the tens place (20) and five in the ones place. Have them add 28 to 12 and discuss the trading that needs to take place.

Focus on Odd and Even
- Build numbers on the abacus. Discuss which numbers are odd and which are even and how they could tell by looking at the number of cereal pieces in the ones place.

Focus on Decimals
- For older children, use the frosting to attach a red hot to the far left of the abacus, representing a decimal. Have students identify the place values (tenths, hundredths, thousandths) and read and write numbers involving decimals.

Focus on Problem Solving
Ask questions such as:
- What is the smallest two-digit number you can make with six pieces of cereal?
- What is the largest number you can make with one piece of cereal?
- What are all the different numbers you can make with four pieces of cereal?

Focus on Skip Counting
- Practice skip counting on the abacus. Place one cereal piece on the tens column at a time and have the children count by tens. Place one cereal piece on the hundreds column at a time and have the children count by hundreds, etc.

Focus on Number Bases
- Work in a base-three or five system on the abacus. For example, explain to the children that each column will only hold three cereal pieces and ask them to place two onto the first stirrer to the right, then ask them to add two more pieces of cereal to the abacus. Discuss what happens and how it is similar to and different from our base-ten system.

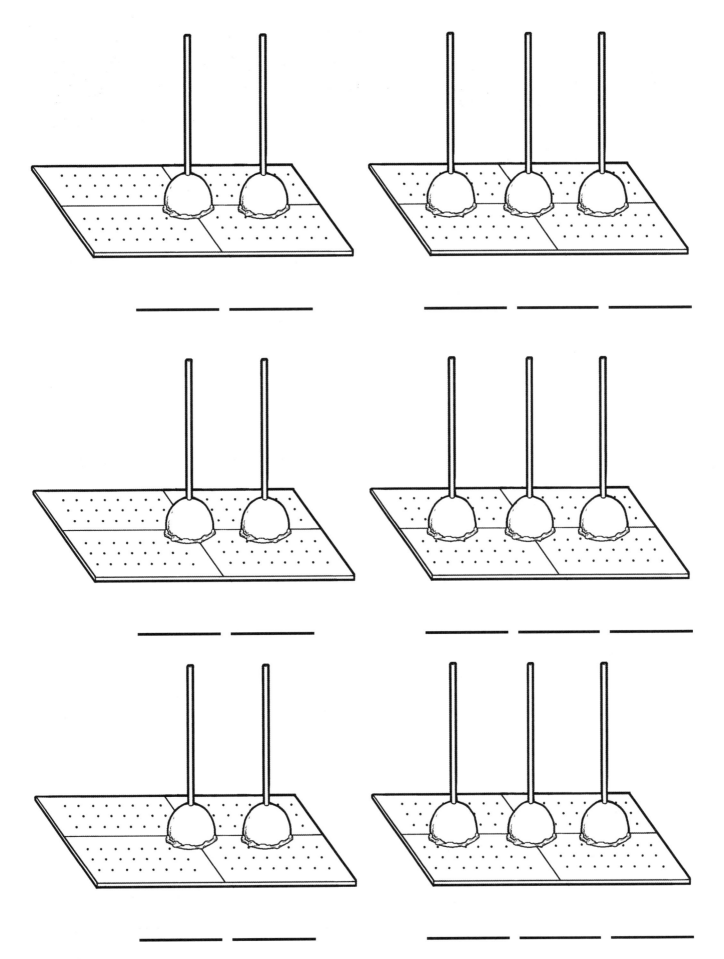

Connecting Learning

1. If Chaun were holding up two toes and three fingers, how many boxes would his father have counted?

2. What is the value of five in the ones place?

3. What is the value of three in the tens place?

4. What is the largest number you could make with three stirrers and six pieces of cereal?

5. How does an abacus work?

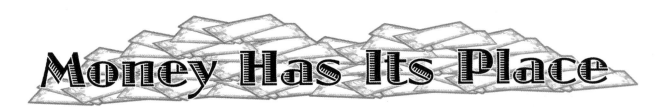

Money Has Its Place

Topic
Operations

Key Question
How can we use our *Operation Boards* to do addition and subtraction problems with money?

Learning Goal
Students will construct manipulative models to represent operations of addition and subtraction of money using one-, two-, and three-digit numbers.

Guiding Document
*NCTM Standards 2000**
- *Use a variety of methods and tools to compute, including objects, mental computation, estimation, paper and pencil, and calculators*
- *Understand various meanings of addition and subtraction of whole numbers and the relationship between the two operations*
- *Understand the effects of adding and subtracting whole numbers*
- *Develop a sense of whole numbers and represent and use them in flexible ways, including relating, composing, and decomposing numbers*
- *Connect number words and numerals to the quantities they represent, using various physical models and representations*

Math
Number and operations
    addition
    subtraction

Integrated Processes
Observing
Recording
Comparing and contrasting
Communicating
Applying

Materials
For each student:
    Operation Boards
    money (see *Management 1*)
    Place Value Labels

Background Information
Building models of numbers and depicting operations using manipulatives help learners build an understanding of the complicated procedures of grouping and regrouping used in operations. This lesson takes the students through a step by step process in which they build models, move objects, and find solutions to addition and subtraction problems.

Money is used in this experience for its real-world application. This activity uses pennies, dimes, and dollars. This relates to the ones, tens, and hundreds used in other place value experiences. The grouping of 10 pennies into a set that can be traded for a dime helps build the understanding for the need for regrouping. Placing these coins on an *Operation Board* labeled in ones, tens, and hundreds continues to build a knowledge base of place value. Using the manipulatives on an *Operation Board*, combined with recording, helps the students begin to build a relationship between the numbers and the placement of these numbers related to place value.

Management
1. Copy enough coins and bills for each student based on the equations being taught at the time.
2. Have the students use the grid to record the addition and subtraction problems with money.

	3	.	8	9
+	1	.	0	7
	4	.	9	6

Procedure
Part One—Addition With Money
1. Give the students yellow, blue, and green *Operation Boards*, *Place Value Labels*, and coins and dollar bills. Direct them to position the boards with the pink section at the bottom. Ask them to place *ones*, *tens*, and *hundreds* labels above the appropriate boards. Direct them to place one penny beside the ones label, one dime beside the tens label, and one dollar beside the hundreds label.

AWESOME ADDITION AND SUPER SUBTRACTION   © 2010 AIMS Education Foundation

2. Give the students a problem to solve such as: Emma had one dollar and three dimes. She found three dimes and six pennies. How much money does she now have?
3. Direct the students to place the money in the correct sections on the *Operation Boards*. Tell them to combine the sections and move the coins to the pink section of their *Operation Boards*. Have them record the actions on the answer grid sheet.
4. Direct the students to work this problem on their *Operation Boards:* Juan had three dollars and 75 cents. He earned five dollars and 55 cents. How much can he now deposit into his savings account?
5. Ask the students what they needed to do in this problem that was different than the first problem. [This problem requires regrouping both in the ones place and the tens place.]
6. Work additional problems involving the addition of money with and without regrouping.

Part Two—Subtraction With Money
1. Give the students yellow, blue, and green *Operation Boards, Place Value Labels,* and coins and dollar bills. Direct them to position the boards with the pink section at the top. Ask them to place *ones, tens,* and *hundreds* labels above the appropriate boards. Direct them to place one penny beside the ones label, one dime beside the tens label, and one dollar beside the hundreds label.
2. Give the students the following problem to solve. Lakeshia had seven dollars and 39 cents. She bought a magazine that cost two dollars and 25 cents. How much does she have left?
3. Have the students place the seven dollars and 39 cents in the pink section. Ask them to move two dollars and 25 cents into the middle section. Tell students to move the remaining money into the bottom section and record the actions on the answer grid sheet.
4. Present the students with the following problem: Jacob has six dollars. He spends four dollars and 86 cents at the school store. How much does he have left?
5. Tell the students to place six dollars in the top pink section of their *Operation Boards*. Inform them that they will need to subtract four dollars and 86 cents from the six dollars. Point out that in subtraction and addition we begin in the ones place. Ask them how we can take six away from nothing. If no one suggests it, point out that they can trade one of the dollars for 10 dimes and one of the dimes for 10 pennies. Guide them in the recording of this process on the answer grid.
6. Work additional problems involving subtracting of money with and without regrouping.

Connecting Learning
1. How are pennies, dimes, and dollars related to place value?
2. What do you need to do when you have more than nine pennies in the ones place or nine dimes in the tens place?
3. Why is it important to look for + and − symbols before trying to work a problem?
4. When you have a four in the hundreds place, zero in the tens place, and you need to subtract three tens from it, what do you need to do?
5. Build a number story using money on your board and then write the number story using numerals. Share your story with someone and have him or her solve the problem

* Reprinted with permission from *Principles and Standards for School Mathematics,* 2000 by the National Council of Teachers of Mathematics. All rights reserved.

Money Has Its Place

Key Question

How can we use our *Operation Boards* to do addition and subtraction problems with money?

Learning Goal

Students will:

construct manipulative models to represent operations of addition and subtraction of money using one-, two-, and three-digit numbers.

Money Has Its Place

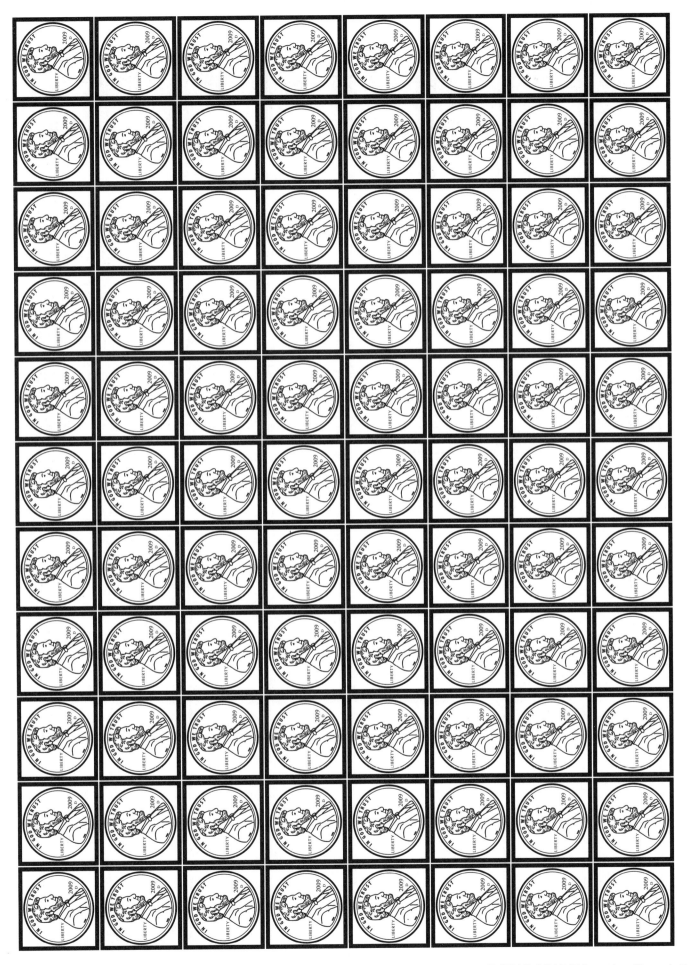

AWESOME ADDITION AND SUPER SUBTRACTION

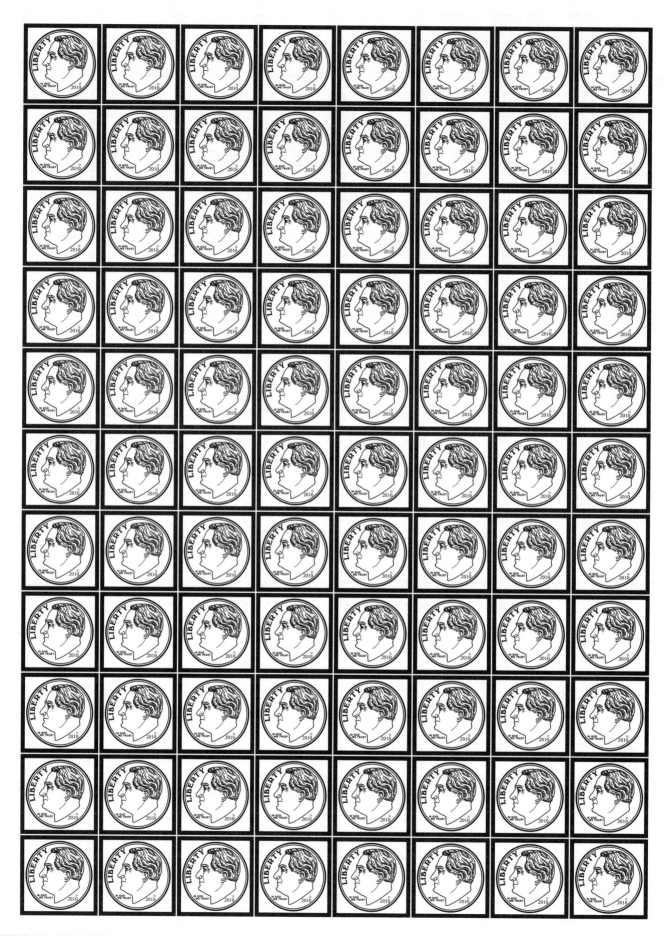

Money Has Its Place

Connecting Learning

1. How are pennies, dimes, and dollars related to place value?

2. What do you need to do when you have more than nine pennies in the ones place or nine dimes in the tens place?

3. Why is it important to look for + and – symbols before trying to work a problem?

4. When you have a four in the hundreds place, zero in the tens place, and you need to subtract three tens from it, what do you need to do?

5. Build a number story using money on your board and then write the number story using numerals. Share your story with someone and have him or her solve the problem.

Meaningful Problem Solving

Big Ideas in Problem Solving

- Patterns are key
- Process is the focus
- Multiple methods should be tried
- Persistence must be developed
- Divergent thinking is important

Problem-Solving Strategies

- Use logical thinking
- Write a number sentence
- Look for patterns
- Guess and check
- Use manipulatives
- Wish for an easier problem
- Organize the information
- Draw out the problem
- Work backwards

Shape Frame Math

Topic
Problem solving

Key Questions
1. How can you determine what numbers belong in the squares based on the number of manipulatives in the hexagon, triangle, and circle?
2. How can you determine the number of manipulatives that belong in the triangle, hexagon, and circle based on the numbers in the squares?

Learning Goals
Students will:
* create an addition problem using the *Shape Frame Math* mat,
* use problem-solving skills to solve for missing addends on their classmates' mats, and
* look for patterns in their mats and in the mats of their classmates.

Guiding Document
NCTM Standards 2000
* *Count with understanding and recognize "how many" in sets of objects*
* *Connect number words and numerals to the quantities they represent, using various physical models and representations*
* *Develop and use strategies for whole-number computations, with a focus on addition and subtraction*

Math
Number and operations
    addition
    odd and even
Problem solving
Patterns

Integrated Processes
Observing
Collecting and recording data
Interpreting data
Comparing and contrasting

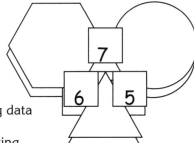

Materials
For each student:
    Shape Frame Math mat
    Shape Frame Math solutions page
    10 or more small manipulatives (see *Management 1*)
    sheet protector (see *Management 3*)
    dry erase marker
    paper towel

Background Information
This activity gives students the opportunity to practice their addition and subtraction skills in a problem-solving setting. They begin by placing manipulatives in three spaces on a page. The sums of the manipulatives in adjacent spaces are written in the box between those spaces. When the manipulatives are removed, the challenge becomes to determine the number of manipulatives that belong in each space, a task that is not so simple as it might seem. This activity is from Robert Wirtz and CDA Math and is used with permission.

Management
1. Students will need at least 10 manipulatives to put in the spaces on the *Shape Frame Math* mat. These manipulatives should be small enough to fit in the spaces and be easily counted. Items such as beans, buttons, or pennies all work well.
2. If you are working with young learners, give them only 10 manipulatives. Increase the number of manipulatives according to the addition skills of your students.
3. Place a *Shape Frame Math* mat in a sheet protector for each student. Students can use the dry erase markers to record their answers and wipe them clean for each new problem. You can also laminate the mats or give students small sticky notes on which to write the sums so that they can be removed for each new problem.
4. This game format is designed to practice addition at the problem-solving level. Use it multiple times throughout the year for extended practice.

Procedure
Part One
1. Give each student a *Shape Frame Math* mat, a dry erase marker, a paper towel, and some manipulatives.
2. Direct them to place a different number of manipulatives in each large shape: hexagon, circle, and triangle.
3. Tell the students to add the number of manipulatives in the hexagon to the number of manipulatives in the triangle and to record this sum in the square that overlaps both these shapes.
4. Direct the students to do the same with the other shapes, recording the sums in the overlapping squares.
5. Tell them to remove the manipulatives, leaving only the recorded sums in the squares.

AWESOME ADDITION AND SUPER SUBTRACTION   55   © 2010 AIMS Education Foundation

6. Have students trade their mats with other classmates. Challenge them to determine the missing manipulatives, or addends, based on the recorded answers. If their numbers add up correctly, they have solved the problem.
7. Continue this process, having students exchange mats with different classmates.
8. Challenge the students to mentally solve for the missing addends.

Part Two
1. Continue the learning game as described in *Part One*, adding the element of keeping a record of each solution. Give each student a *Shape Frame Math* solutions page.
2. Direct the students to record their challenge problems and solutions on the *Shape Frame Math* solutions pages.
3. Discuss any patterns or similarities they notice among the problems and solutions.

Connecting Learning
1. What method(s) did you use to solve the problems?
2. How does this compare to your classmates' methods? Are they the same or different?
3. Were some problems easier to solve? ...harder to solve? Why?
4. What did you do to solve the problems when the manipulatives were not available?
5. Look at the combination of addends used in the three large shapes on each of the problems. Describe what you see. Do you find any that are all even? ...all odd?
6. Do you think you could design a challenge problem that would work in this format that would include all even addends? [Yes.] ...all odd addends? [Yes.] Explain why. (As long as the students can control the total number of manipulatives that they place in the shapes, they will always be able to make the addends either all odd or all even. If the total number of manipulatives is fixed, then the addends cannot be all even or all odd.)
7. Look at the combination of numbers used in the three squares on each of the problems on the *Shape Frame Math* solutions pages. Do you find any that are all even? ...all odd? Describe what you discover.
8. Do you think you could design a challenge problem that would work in this format that would have three even sums? [Yes.] ...three odd sums? [No.] Explain why. [When all of the addends are even, the result is three even sums. When all of the addends are odd, the result is three even sums. When the addends are both odd and even, the result is two odd sums and one even sum.]

Extensions
1. Older students can be challenged to explore the nature of odd and even numbers. What happens when you add two odd numbers? ...two even numbers? ...an odd and an even number? How does this relate to the problems you were able to create with the mat?
2. Create a mat that has four shapes and repeat the activity. How do these results compare with those from a three-shape mat?

* Reprinted with permission from *Principles and Standards for School Mathematics*, 2000 by National Council of Teachers of Mathematics. All rights reserved.

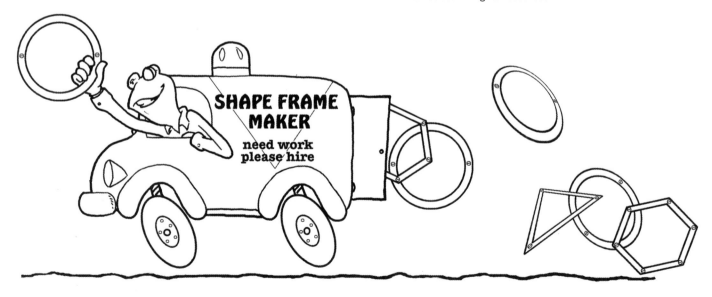

Shape Frame Math

Key Questions

1. How can you determine what numbers belong in the squares based on the number of manipulatives in the hexagon, triangle, and circle?

2. How can you determine the number of manipulatives that belong in the triangle, hexagon, and circle based on the numbers in the squares?

Learning Goals

Students will:

- create an addition problem using the *Shape Frame Math* mat,
- use problem-solving skills to solve for missing addends on their classmates' mats, and
- look for patterns in their mats and in the mats of their classmates.

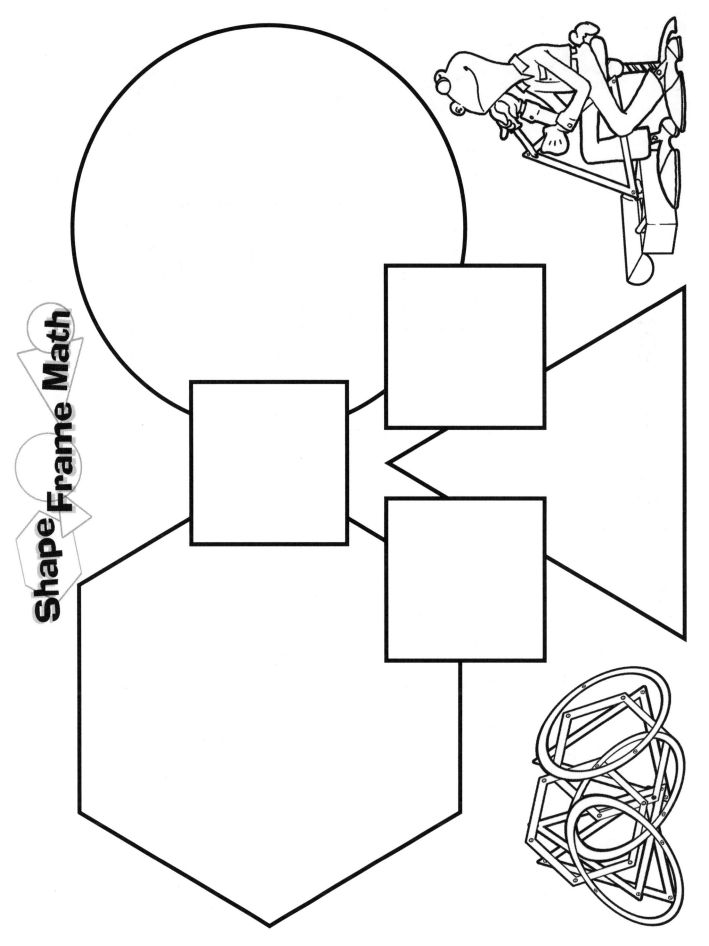

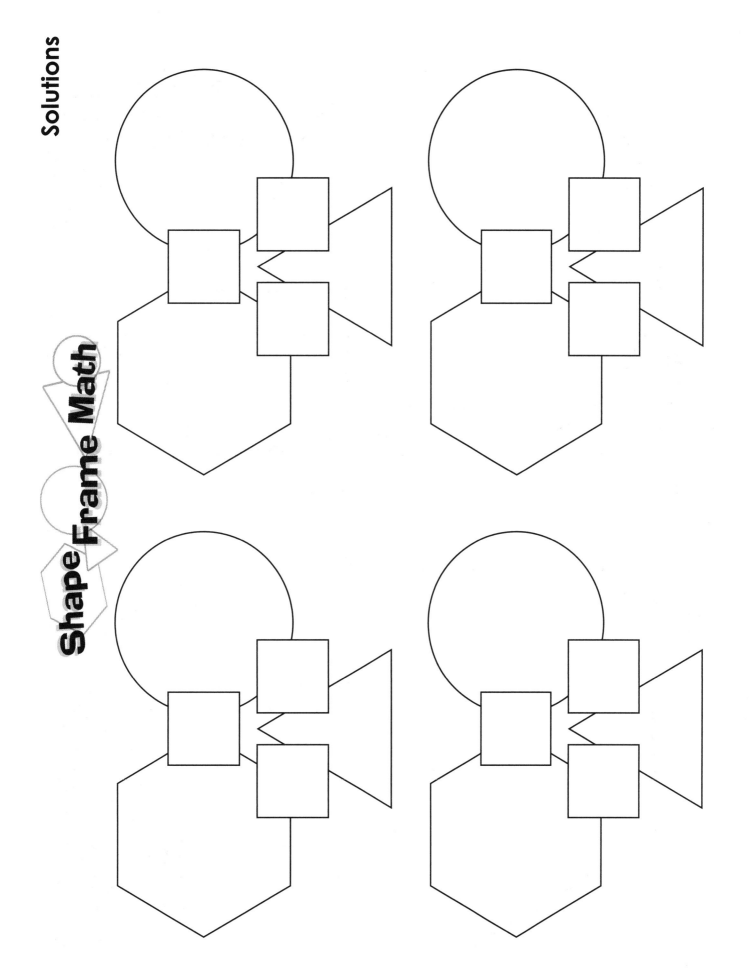

Shape Frame Math

Connecting Learning

1. What method(s) did you use to solve the problems?

2. How does this compare to your classmates' methods? Are they the same or different?

3. Were some problems easier to solve? ...harder to solve? Why?

4. What did you do to solve the problems when the manipulatives were not available?

5. Look at the combination of addends used in the three large shapes on each of the problems. Describe what you see. Do you find any that are all even? ...all odd?

Shape Frame Math

Connecting Learning

6. Do you think you could design a challenge problem that would work in this format that would include all even addends? ...all odd addends? Explain why.

7. Look at the combination of numbers used in the three squares on each of the problems on the *Shape Frame Math* solutions pages. Do you find any that are all even? ...all odd? Describe what you discover.

8. Do you think you could design a challenge problem that would work in this format that would have three even sums? ...three odd sums? Explain why.

Making Arrangements

Topic
Place value

Key Question
How many different ways can you make the number 148 with Base Ten Blocks?

Learning Goals
Students will:
- recognize that groupings of one, tens, and hundreds can be taken apart in several ways; and
- realize there are patterns in the ways that numbers are formed.

Guiding Document
NCTM Standards 2000*
- *Understand numbers, ways of representing numbers, relationships among numbers and number systems*
- *Understand the place-value structure of the base-ten numbers system and be able to represent and compare whole numbers and decimals*
- *Recognize equivalent representations for the same number and generate them by decomposing and composing numbers*

Math
Number sense
    place value
Problem solving

Integrated Processes
Observing
Comparing and contrasting
Organizing

Materials
For each group of students:
    Base Ten Blocks
    pencils
    student page

For the teacher:
    transparency of arrangements recording chart

Background Information
Children often are able to state the proper number of ones, tens, and hundreds, but find it difficult to break a multi-digit number into different arrangements. This activity challenges students to realize that the groupings of ones, tens, and hundreds can be taken apart in several ways.

Procedure
1. Distribute the student page and Base Ten Blocks to pairs or trios of students.
2. Ask a student to build the number 148 with the Base Ten Blocks.
3. Have several students share some other possible arrangements.
4. In small groups of two and three, have students build the number and record their arrangements on the student page until they find *all* possible arrangements.
5. As they are building and recording, encourage groups to share observations and try to discover patterns in their arrangements.

Connecting Learning
1. How many different arrangements are there? [20] How do you know if you have all the possible solutions? [There are various patterns to the different arrangements.]
2. What are some of the patterns found in the chart? [There are consecutive counting numbers in the tens place (0–4 are used twice). There are possible block totals from 13–148. There are differences of nine blocks used in each total.]
3. What do you suppose would happen to the total number of arrangements if the digit in the ones place were raised or lowered? …the digit in the tens or the hundreds place?

AWESOME ADDITION AND SUPER SUBTRACTION   63   © 2010 AIMS Education Foundation

Solutions

Number 148

Groups of Hundreds	Groups of Tens	Groups of Ones	Total # of Blocks
1	0	48	49
1	1	38	40
1	2	28	31
1	3	18	22
1	4	8	13
0	0	148	148
0	1	138	139
0	2	128	130
0	3	118	121
0	4	108	112
0	5	98	103
0	6	88	94
0	7	78	85
0	8	68	76
0	9	58	67
0	10	48	58
0	11	38	49
0	12	28	40
0	13	18	31
0	14	8	22

* Reprinted with permission from *Principles and Standards for School Mathematics,* 2000 by the National Council of Teachers of Mathematics. All rights reserved.

Making Arrangements

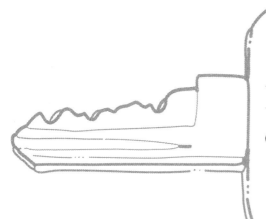

Key Question

How many different ways can you make the number 148 with Base Ten Blocks?

Learning Goals

Students will:

- recognize that groupings of one, tens, and hundreds can be taken apart in several ways; and

- realize there are patterns in the ways that numbers are formed.

Making Arrangements

NUMBER _____

GROUPS OF HUNDREDS	GROUPS OF TENS	GROUPS OF ONES	TOTAL NUMBER OF BLOCKS

AWESOME ADDITION AND SUPER SUBTRACTION © 2010 AIMS Education Foundation

Making Arrangements

Connecting Learning

1. How many different arrangements are there? How do you know if you have all the possible solutions?

2. What are some of the patterns found in the chart?

3. What do you suppose would happen to the total number of arrangements if the digit in the ones place were raised or lowered? …the digit in the tens or the hundreds place?

MATH SPOTS

Topic
Problem solving

Key Question
How can you arrange numbers in a variety of arrays so that each line equals a specific target sum?

Learning Goals
Students will:
- use problem-solving skills to arrange numbers so that they total a target sum,
- gain practice using addition to solve problems, and
- look for patterns in their solutions.

Guiding Document
NCTM Standards 2000*
- *Develop fluency with basic number combinations for addition and subtraction*
- *Understand the effects of adding and subtracting whole numbers*
- *Develop and use strategies for whole-number computations, with a focus on addition and subtraction*

Math
Number and operations
    addition
Patterns
Problem solving

Integrated Processes
Observing
Comparing and contrasting
Collecting and recording data
Interpreting data

Materials
For each student:
    student pages
    number cards (see *Management 2*)

Background Information
    The challenges in this activity provide the opportunity for students to practice addition in the context of problem solving. The different arrays provide varying levels of difficulty and allow students to gain confidence in their abilities before moving on to more difficult problems. The many possible extensions and patterns present in the solutions make these problems worth revisiting again and again throughout the year.

Management
1. This game format is designed to practice addition at the problem-solving level. Use it multiple times throughout the year for extended practice.
2. Students will need number cards labeled with the numerals one to six. These cards should fit into the spaces on the student pages. Scratch paper cut into small squares works well.
3. There are several different *Math Spots* arrays that vary in difficulty based on their configuration and number of spaces. Choose the arrays that are most appropriate for your students.

Procedure
1. Give each student one of the *Math Spots* pages and a set of number cards.
2. Direct the students to write the appropriate target sum (in pencil) on the line below the array. The possible target sums for the first array are:

8, 9, 10

3. Challenge the students to arrange their number cards in the spaces so that the sum of each line in the array equals the target sum.
4. Once students find a solution, direct them to record it on the appropriate *Math Spots* recording page.
5. Challenge the students to find as many different solutions for this target sum as they can. Have them record their solutions and compare them with other classmates.
6. Assign a second target sum for the array. Have students find as many solutions as they can for this new sum.
7. Continue assigning any remaining target sums.
8. Repeat this process with as many of the different arrays as time allows. This time, however, let students determine the target sums.
9. Close with a time of class discussion in which students look for patterns in their solutions and describe what they find.

Connecting Learning
1. What did you do that helped you solve the problems?
2. How does your strategy compare to the strategies used by your classmates?

AWESOME ADDITION AND SUPER SUBTRACTION   © 2010 AIMS Education Foundation

3. Were some problems easier to solve? ...harder to solve? Why?
4. Do any numbers work as target sums? [No.] Why or why not? [There are only a few possible sums, depending on the arrangement. Different target sums require different numbers to be placed in the arrays.]
5. Does it matter whether or not a target sum is odd or even? [It depends on the array.] How do you know this?
6. Do you think the class has discovered all the possible solutions for each target sum for the different arrays? How can you find out?
7. Look at the solutions on your recording pages. What patterns do you see?

Triangular Array
1. Look at all of the corner numbers. What do you notice?
2. Look at all of the inside numbers. What do you notice?
3. Is nine the smallest sum possible using the numbers one to six? [Yes.] Why? [Since six is the largest number, the lowest sum possible is 6 + 1 + 2 = 9.]
4. Is 12 the largest sum possible using the numbers one to six? [Yes.] Why? [Since one is the smallest number, the highest sum possible is 1 + 5 + 6 = 12.]

Extensions
Use different numbers in the arrays to reach different target sums and compare the solutions for patterns.

Cross Array
1. Use the numbers 2-6 to get target sums of 11 and 13.
2. Use the first five odd numbers to get target sums of 13 and 15.
3. Use the first five even numbers to get target sums of 16 and 18.

Zigzag Array
1. Use the numbers 2-6 to get a target sum of 9.
2. Use the first five even numbers to get target sums of 12 and 14. Is it possible to use the first five odd numbers in this array? Why or why not?

U-shaped Array
1. Use the numbers 2-6 to get a target sum of 9. Why is there only one target sum when the numbers 2-6 are used?
2. Use the first five even numbers to get target sums of 12 and 14. Is it possible to use the first five odd numbers in this array? Why or why not?

Triangular Array
1. Use the numbers 2-7 to get target sums of 12, 13, 14, and 15.
2. Use the first six odd numbers to get target sums of 15, 17, 19, and 21.
3. Use the first six even numbers to get target sums of 18, 20, 22, and 24.

* Reprinted with permission from *Principles and Standards for School Mathematics*, 2000 by National Council of Teachers of Mathematics. All rights reserved.

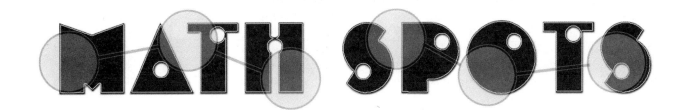

Key Question

How can you arrange numbers in a variety of arrays so that each line equals a specific target sum?

Learning Goals

Students will:

- use problem-solving skills to arrange numbers so that they total a target sum,

- gain practice using addition to solve problems, and

- look for patterns in their solutions.

Arrange the numbers 1, 2, 3, 4, and 5 in the circles so that each line has the same sum.

Target Sum

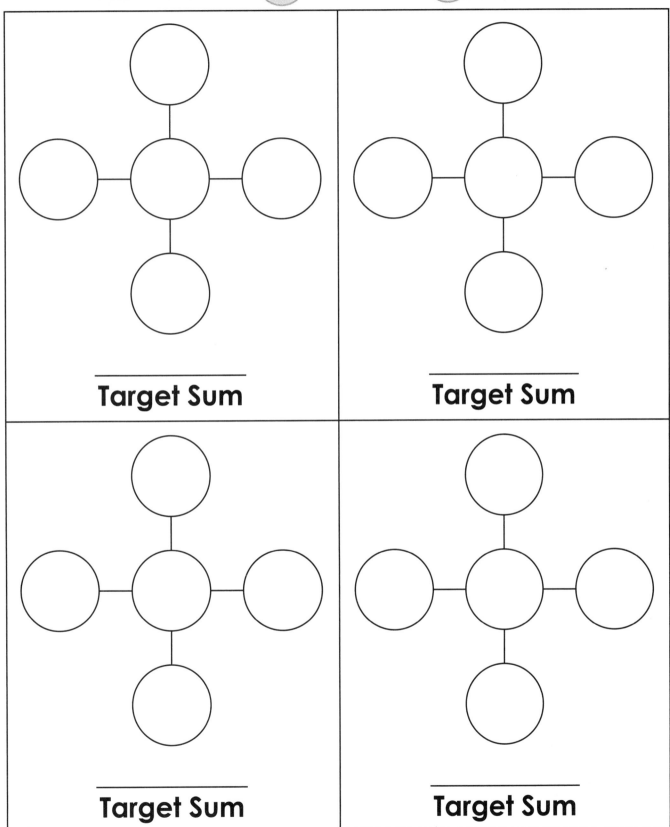

Arrange the numbers 1, 2, 3, 4, and 5 in the circles so that each line has the same sum.

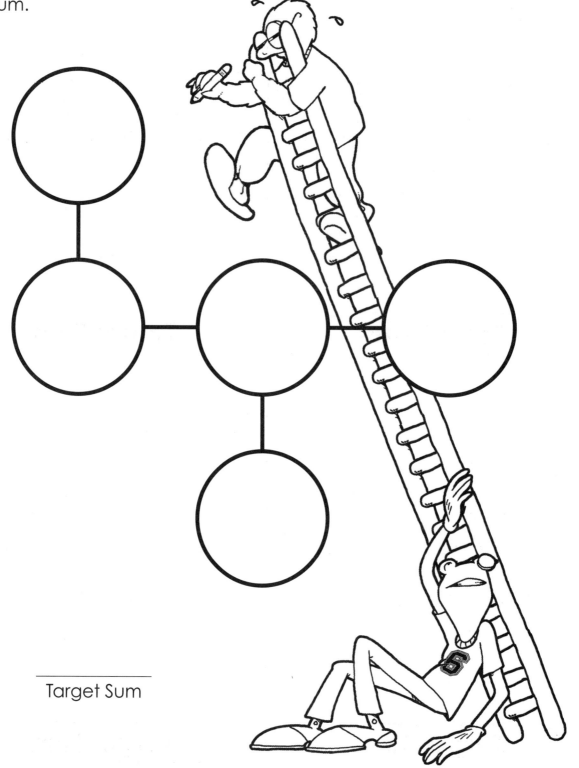

_____
Target Sum

AWESOME ADDITION AND SUPER SUBTRACTION

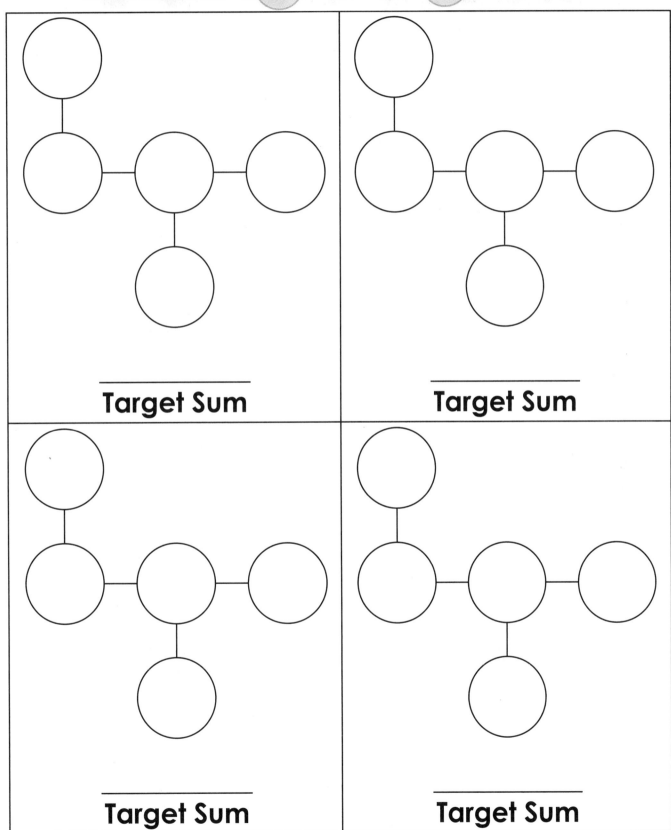

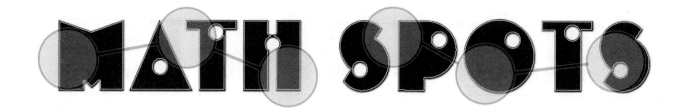

Arrange the numbers 1, 2, 3, 4 and 5 in the circles so that each line has the same sum.

Target Sum

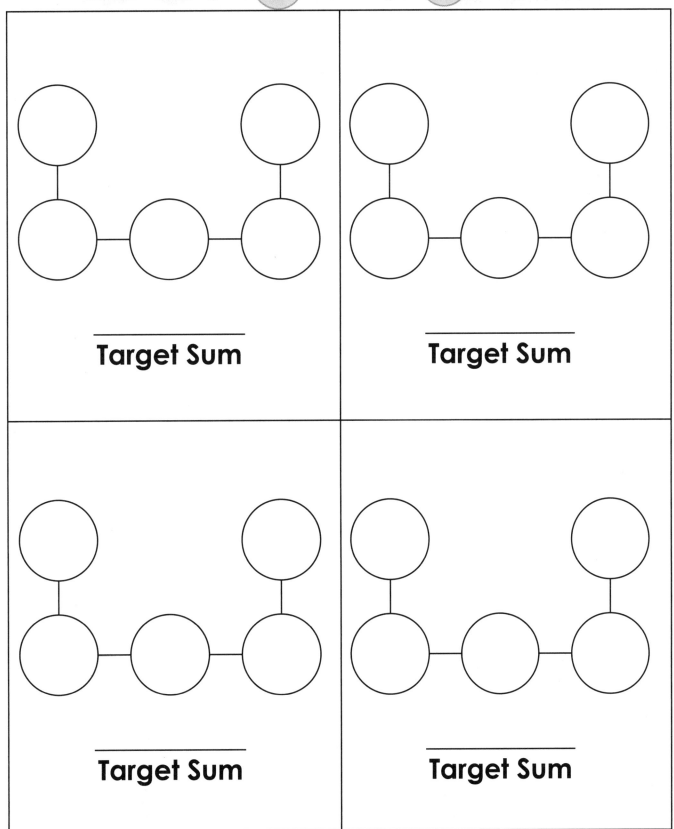

AWESOME ADDITION AND SUPER SUBTRACTION   77   © 2010 AIMS Education Foundation

MATH SPOTS

Arrange the numbers 1, 2, 3, 4, 5 and 6 in the circles so that each line has the same sum.

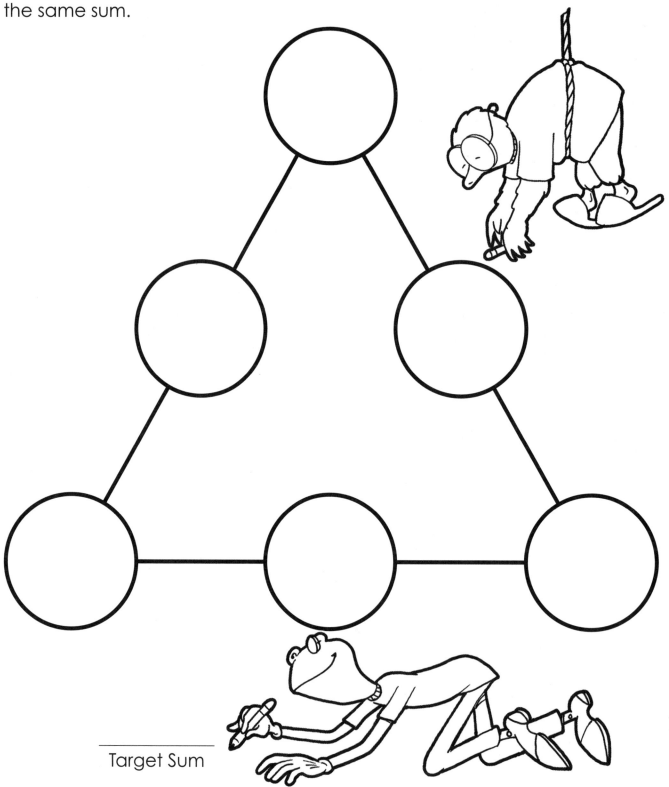

Target Sum

AWESOME ADDITION AND SUPER SUBTRACTION

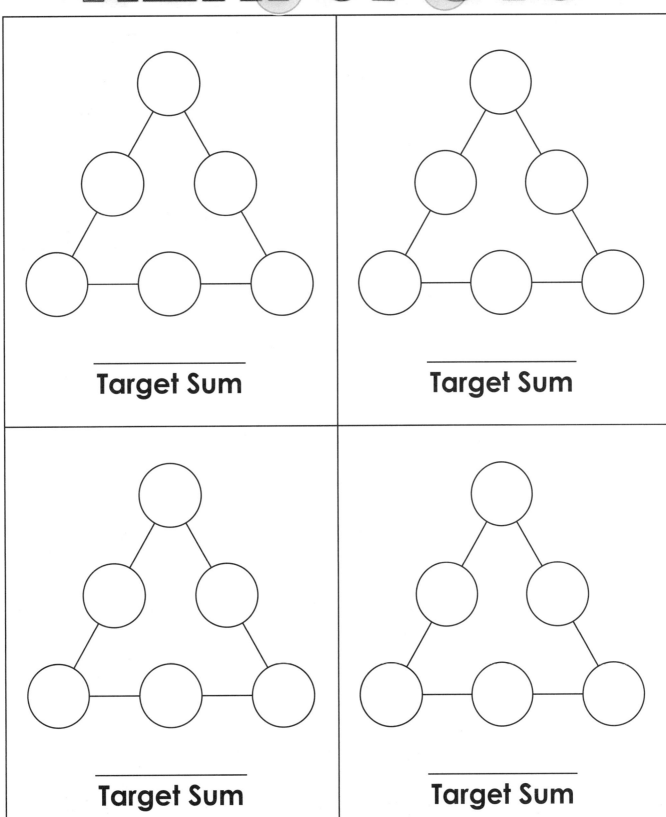

Please use the numbers 1-7. Find a solution in which the sum is the same along each of the lines.

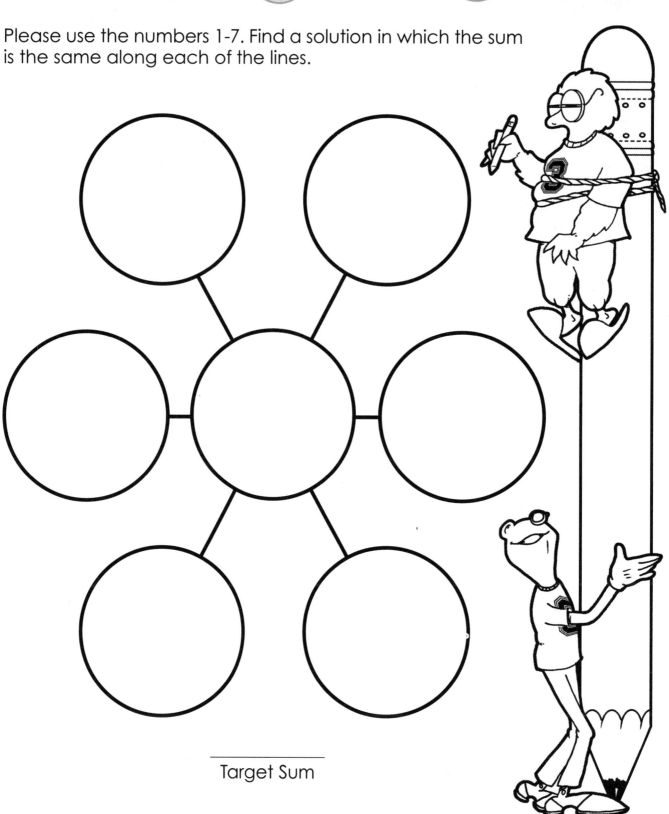

Target Sum

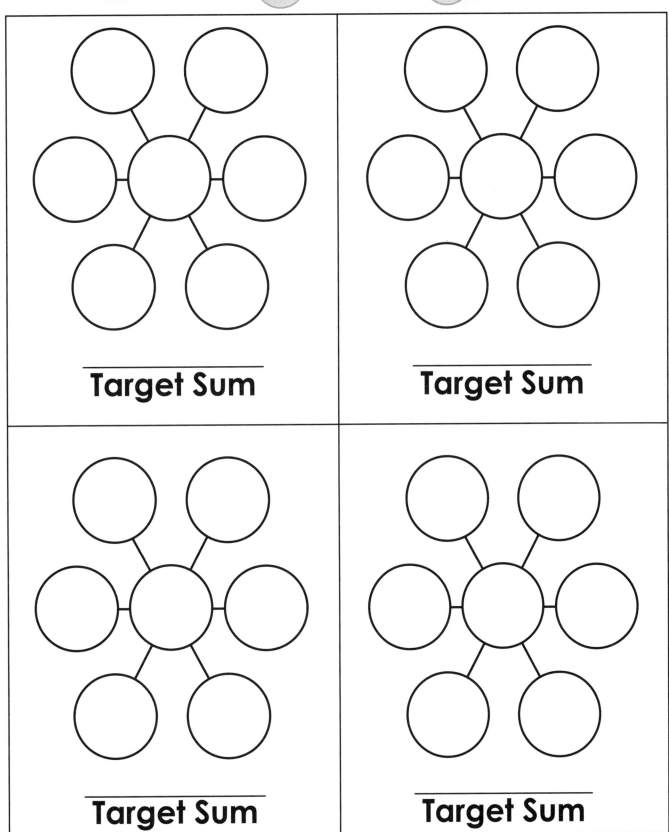

Target Sum

Target Sum

Target Sum

Target Sum

AWESOME ADDITION AND SUPER SUBTRACTION © 2010 AIMS Education Foundation

Please use the numbers 1-9. Find a solution in which the sum is the same along each of the lines.

Target Sum

AWESOME ADDITION AND SUPER SUBTRACTION   82   © 2010 AIMS Education Foundation

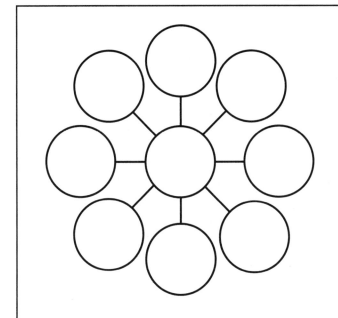

Target Sum

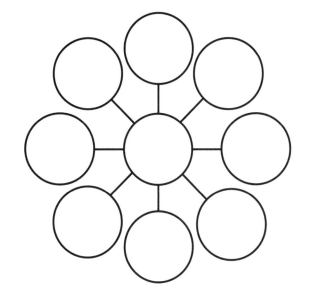

Target Sum

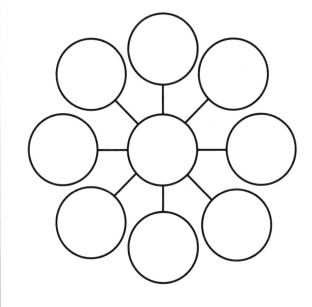

Target Sum

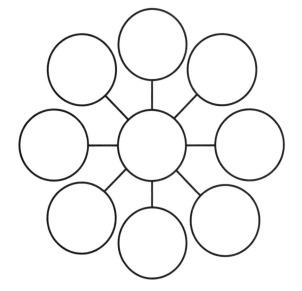

Target Sum

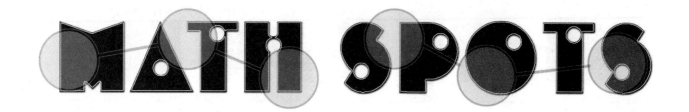

Please use the numbers 1-9. Arrange them so the sum is correct for the two addends.

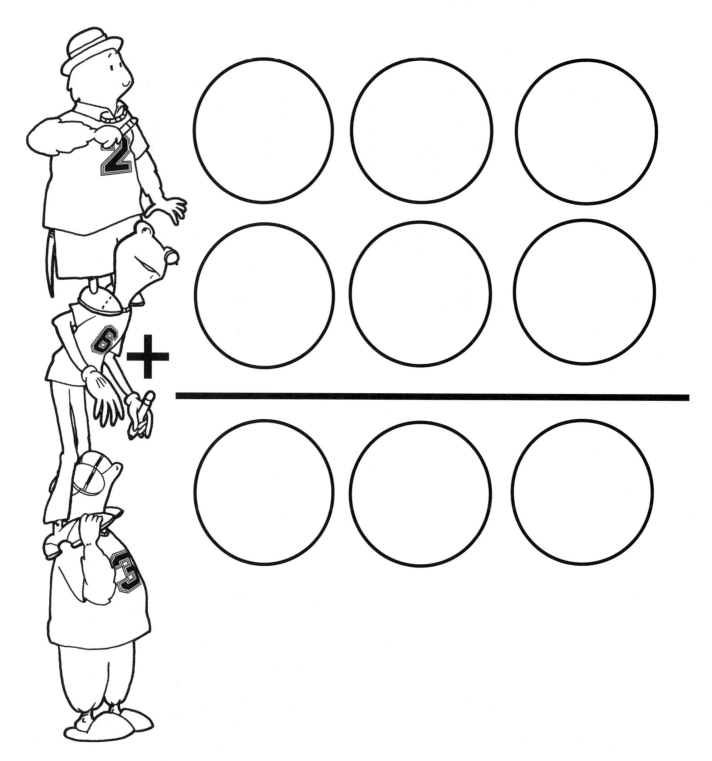

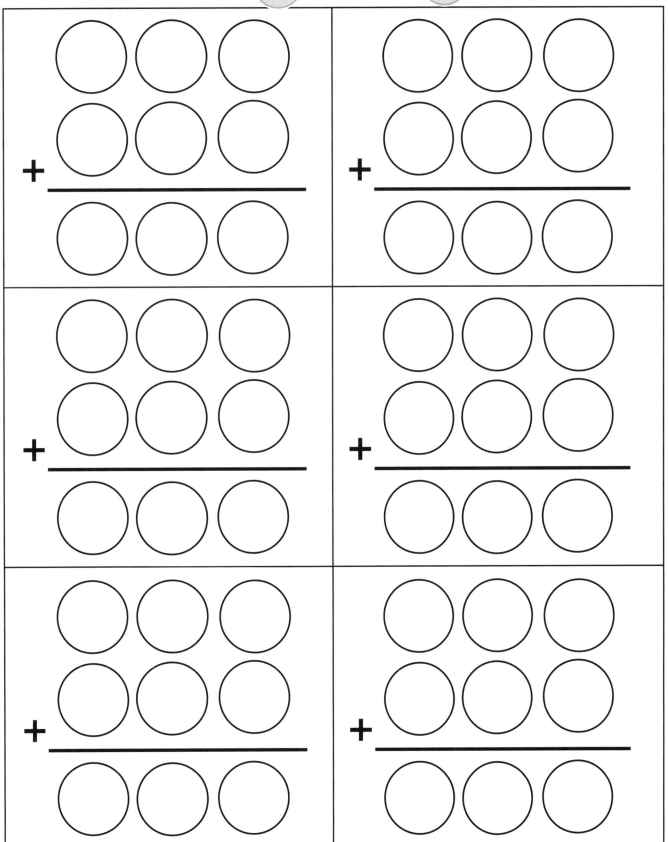

AWESOME ADDITION AND SUPER SUBTRACTION

Connecting Learning

1. What did you do that helped you solve the problems?

2. How does your strategy compare to the strategies used by your classmates?

3. Were some problems easier to solve? ...harder to solve? Why?

4. Do any numbers work as target sums? Why or why not?

5. Does it matter whether or not a target sum is odd or even? How do you know this?

6. Do you think the class has discovered all the possible solutions for each target sum for the different arrays? How can you find out?

7. Look at the solutions on your recording pages. What patterns do you see?

DIVING Into DIFFIES

Directions
To make a diffie, select any four digits from 1 to 9 and write them in a row. Find the difference between each pair and then between the first and last numbers. Record these differences in a row below the first row of numbers. Repeat this process until you get to a row of zeros.

Example

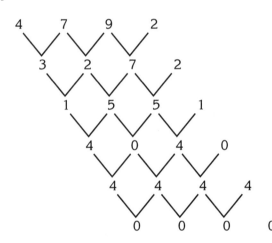

This is an example of a six-level diffie. The sixth row is a row of zeros. Each row is a sequence of differences from the row above.

Procedure
1. Challenge students to design diffies of their own.
2. Post their diffies on the board and compare and contrast their solutions.
3. Use the *Connecting Learning* questions as a guide and as inspiration for further exploration.

Connecting Learning
1. How many levels were you able to get?
2. How does your diffie compare to others that have the same number of levels?
3. What does the largest diffie that we found look like?
4. What patterns do you notice in the diffies?
5. What happens if you include zero?
6. What would happen if you put five numbers in a row?
7. Could you do this with numbers with double digits?

From CDA Math by Robert Wirtz. Used by permission.

DIAMOND DIFFIES

Directions
Diamond Diffies offer an opportunity for students to use their knowledge of the basic subtraction facts in a playful, intelligent way. Begin by writing a number in each of the four circles in the corners of the array. Find the difference between each pair of corner numbers and write it in the circle between them. For example, with starting numbers of 17, 12, 3, and 7, the differences would be 5, 14, 5, and 4 as shown.

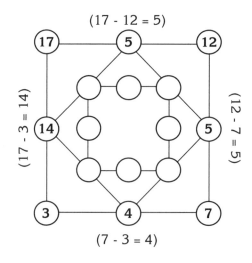

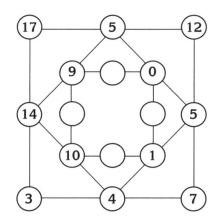

Now, find the differences between these new pairs of numbers. Again, record the difference in the circle between the two numbers as shown.

Repeat this process once more until all the circles are filled.

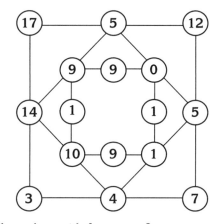

Procedure
1. Distribute the first student page and explain to students the process for completing these *Diamond Diffies*.
2. Encourage students to investigate questions that arise as they work on the problems and to keep records of their investigations.

Connecting Learning
1. If you kept finding differences long enough, would all arrays eventually end up with four zeros?
2. Is there any way to predict how many times you must find the differences before the four differences are all zeros?
3. How are these diffies like the ones you did with a row of numbers? How are they different?
4. What do you think would happen if you tried a triangular diffie?

From CDA Math by Robert Wirtz. Used by permission.

AWESOME ADDITION AND SUPER SUBTRACTION © 2010 AIMS Education Foundation

DIAMOND DIFFIES

Start with a number in each corner and work toward the center.

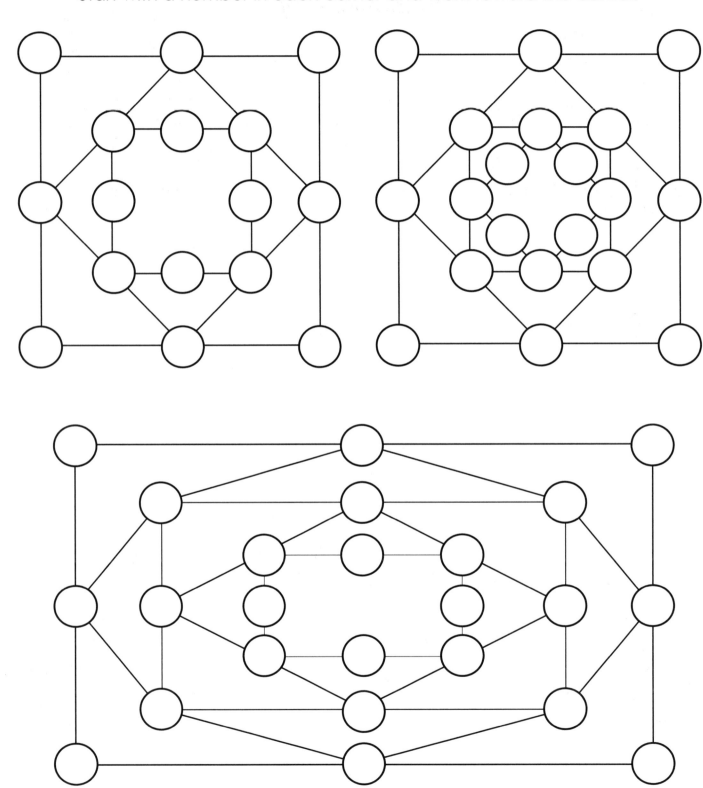

AWESOME ADDITION AND SUPER SUBTRACTION © 2010 AIMS Education Foundation

DIAMOND DIFFIES

Triangular Diffy

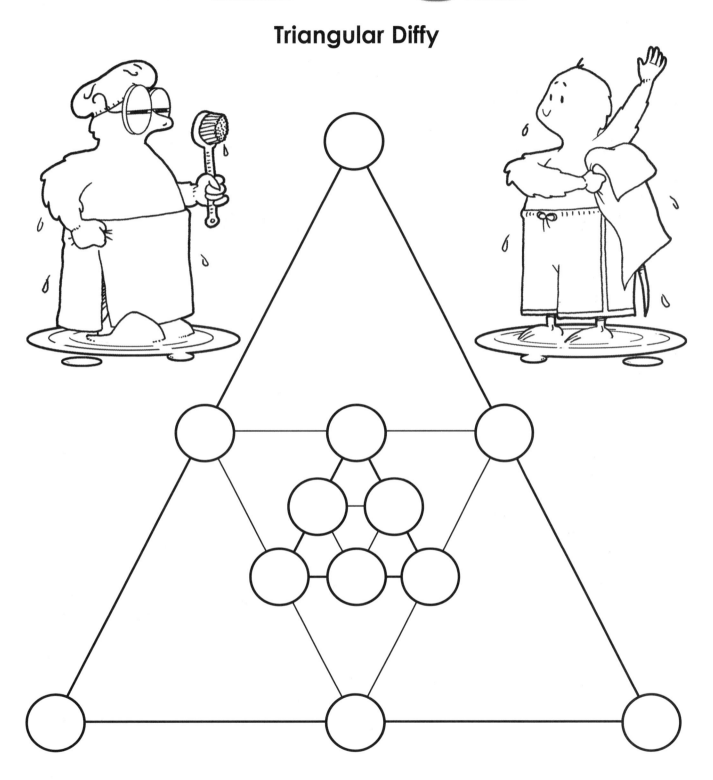

Digits in Disguise

Topic
Problem solving

Key Question
How can you solve number riddles using a series of clues?

Learning Goals
Students will:
* work in groups to solve number riddles, and
* use the language of mathematics to create number riddles of their own for their classmates to solve.

Guiding Document
*NCTM Standards 2000**
* *Use the language of mathematics to express mathematical ideas precisely*
* *Build new mathematical knowledge through problem solving*
* *Apply and adapt a variety of appropriate strategies to solve problems*
* *Monitor and reflect on the process of mathematical problem solving*

Math
Problem solving
Number and operations
   addition
   subtraction
   odd and even
Number sense
   place value
   equalities and inequalities
      greater than/less than

Integrated Processes
Observing
Comparing and contrasting
Recording
Communicating

Materials
Student pages
Sticky notes, optional

Background Information
Digits in Disguise is an adaptation of a language arts activity called "Who am I?" This activity, from Bob and Marlene McCracken (consultants in reading and writing), was intended to help students become better at using descriptive language in their writing. In the first part of the activity, students picked a character from a book they were reading and then listed as many adjectives and/or phrases as they could describing that character. In the second part, students used this list to come up with several statements describing the character, without saying the character's name. These statements were incorporated into a riddle of sorts. However, the goal of this riddle was not to stump its readers, but to help them know exactly which character was being described. For example, if students were reading *Charlotte's Web,* the statements (riddle) describing Charlotte might be:

    I saved a friend's life.
    I created quite a stir with my evening's work.
    I am not afraid of heights.
    I have a soft spot for porcine pets.
    I am a skilled weaver.
    Who am I?

After writing and refining these riddles, students used construction paper and marking pens to make nice copies for placement on a bulletin board. The line with the question "Who am I?" was written on a narrow strip of different-colored construction paper that was as long as the larger piece of construction paper was wide. A piece of tape was put along the top of this strip and attached to the construction paper so that it served as a flap hiding the solution, which was written at the bottom of the paper. The completed riddles were pinned to the bulletin board and students went there and read the riddles in their free time. After reading each riddle, they guessed the solution and lifted the flap to see if they were correct.

This activity changes the final question to "What number am I?" and has students creating their own number riddles. This provides an excellent opportunity for students to think and communicate mathematically.

Management
1. Three different pages with riddles have been included that are aimed at different ability levels. Pick the riddles that are most appropriate for your students and either write them on the board or run off copies and give them to your students. These riddles are intended to be done in groups, but you may choose to give them to individual students instead.

2. An optional fourth student page is included to distribute if you choose to have students write their own riddles individually. You will need a supply of sticky notes for this section so that students can cover up their numbers. After they have written their riddles, they can trade papers with each other and try to solve other students' riddles. The riddles can then be placed on a bulletin board so that everyone has access to them.
3. Students need plenty of practice describing numbers using correct mathematical statements before they are asked to write number riddles. Students need to be reminded that a good riddle is one that leads the reader to the correct answer, not one that stumps the reader. Be sure to assess students' readiness before having them create their riddles.

Procedure
1. Tell students that you are going to test their math skills with some riddles. You will give them clues and they will have to tell you the number described by the clues.
2. Pick several numbers and write statements describing each number on the board as shown in the following example:
   I am less than 20.
   I am an even number.
   My tens digit is one.
   The sum of my two digits is nine.
   What number am I? [18]
3. After doing several examples together as a class, distribute one or more of the pages of riddles and have students work in groups to solve the riddles.
4. Once students are comfortable solving the riddles, challenge groups of students to pick a number and create a number riddle describing that number. Go from group to group facilitating this process by giving hints when needed without doing students' thinking for them. (This interaction will give you insight into students' thinking and help you assess their numeracy skills.)
5. As each group finishes writing a riddle, put it on the board for others to see. Solve each of the riddles together as a class. (During this process, students will see how other groups described their numbers, thereby exposing everyone in the class to a variety of mathematical language.)
6. If appropriate for your students, distribute the fourth student page and sticky notes, and have individual students create and share their own number riddles.
7. Close the activity with a time of sharing and class discussion.

Connecting Learning
1. How were you able to solve the number riddles?
2. Were some riddles harder to solve than others? Explain.
3. Which clues were most helpful in solving the number riddles? Why?
4. How did you decide on the clues to use in your group's riddle?
5. Were others able to solve your group's number riddle? Why or why not?

Solutions
I am odd. I am less than 10. I am greater than 7. [9]

I am even. I am greater than 10. I am less than 14. [12]

I am between 5 and 12. I am odd. I have two digits. [11]

I have two digits. I am an odd number. Both of my digits are the same. I am greater than 80. [99]

I am a two-digit number. I am less than 60. My digits are consecutive numbers. The sum of my digits is 11. [56]

I have three digits. I am greater than 500 and less than 600. My tens and ones digits are both the same even number. The sum of all my digits is nine. [522]

I am less than 100. I am an odd number. My tens digit is three greater than my ones digit. The sum of my two digits is nine. [63]

I have two digits. The sum of my two digits is 10. My tens digit is four more than my ones digit. I am greater than 50. [73]

I have three digits. I am a multiple of five. My hundreds digit is four less than my ones digit. My tens digit is 3. I am less than 200. [135]

* Reprinted with permission from *Principles and Standards for School Mathematics*, 2000 by the National Council of Teachers of Mathematics. All rights reserved.

Digits in Disguise

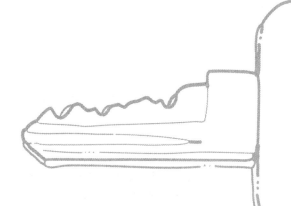

Key Question

How can you solve number riddles using a series of clues?

Learning Goals

Students will:

- work in groups to solve number riddles, and

- use the language of mathematics to create number riddles of their own for their classmates to solve.

Digits in Disguise

Try to solve the following number riddles.
Show your work.

I am odd.
I am less than 10.
I am greater than 7.

_____

I am even.
I am greater than 10.
I am less than 14.

_____

I am between 5 and 12.
I am odd.
I have two digits.

_____

AWESOME ADDITION AND SUPER SUBTRACTION

Digits in Disguise

Try to solve the following number riddles.
Show your work.

I have two digits.
I am an odd number.
Both of my digits are the same.
I am greater than 80.

I am a two-digit number.
I am less than 60.
My digits are consecutive numbers.
The sum of my digits is 11.

I have three digits.
I am greater than 500 and less than 600.
My tens and ones digits are both the same even number.
The sum of all my digits is nine.

Digits in Disguise

Try to solve the following number riddles. Show your work. You may need to use the back of the paper.

I am less than 100.
I am an odd number.
My tens digit is three greater than my ones digit.
The sum of my two digits is nine.

_____

I have two digits.
The sum of my two digits is 10.
My tens digit is four more than my ones digit.
I am greater than 50.

_____

I have three digits.
I am a multiple of five.
My hundreds digit is four less than my ones digit.
My tens digit is 3.
I am less than 200.

_____

Digits in Disguise

Create a number riddle by following these instructions:

1. Choose a number for your riddle. Write it on the line at the bottom of the paper and cover it with a sticky note.

2. Write several clues describing your number on the lines provided.

3. Trade papers with a classmate and see if he or she can guess your number.

RIDDLE OF THE VOLE
answer correctly you may pass

Clues
_____
_____
_____
_____
_____

What number am I?
_____

AWESOME ADDITION AND SUPER SUBTRACTION © 2010 AIMS Education Foundation

Digits in Disguise

Connecting Learning

1. How were you able to solve the number riddles?

2. Were some riddles harder to solve than others? Explain.

3. Which clues were most helpful in solving the number riddles? Why?

4. How did you decide on the clues to use in your group's riddle?

5. Were others able to solve your group's number riddle? Why or why not?

Clear the Deck

Purpose of the Game
Pairs or groups of students will work together to take away all of the cards before getting five tally marks.

Materials
Die
Playing cards (see *Management 2*)

Management
1. This game can be played with two to four players.
2. Each group of students needs the one (ace) through nine in all four suits from a deck of cards.

Directions
1. Shuffle the cards and place them face down in six stacks of four.
2. Turn the top card on each stack face up.
3. Roll the die. Take away any card or combination of cards that equals the number on the die.
4. All players work together to determine the best play. Addition and/or subtraction can be used. A maximum of three cards can be removed in one turn. For example, if a five is rolled, cards that could be removed include a five; a six and one ($6 - 1 = 5$); a two and a three ($2 + 3 = 5$); a four, a two, and an ace ($4 + 2 - 1 = 5$); etc. When the top card is removed from a stack, the card beneath it is turned over.
5. If a card or cards cannot be found to equal the number on the die, players make a tally mark. Play continues until there are no more cards or five tally marks are made.

Uncle Rebus Stories

Topic
Whole number operations

Key Question
How can we solve a variety of story problems?

Learning Goals
Students will:
- identify problems to be solved in stories; and
- solve problems using words, pictures, and/or symbols.

Guiding Document
NCTM Standards 2000*
- *Use multiple models to develop initial understandings of place value and the base-ten number system*
- *Develop a sense of whole numbers and represent and use them in flexible ways, including relating, composing, and decomposing numbers*
- *Connect number words and numerals to the quantities they represent, using various physical models and representations*
- *Understand various meanings of addition and subtraction of whole numbers and the relationship between the two operations*

Math
Whole number operations
  story problems

Integrated Processes
Observing
Comparing and contrasting
Relating
Communicating
Applying

Materials
For each group of students:
  two brown bags
  character page
  number page
  story problem pages
  crayon or highlighter pen
  glue stick

Frank Frog

Background Information
Students often have a difficult time solving story problems. They may benefit from directed instruction that focuses their attention on the problem's components and what the problem is actually asking. The problems presented in this experience are representative of the types often encountered by students. In each story, students are first asked to identify and underline the problem the story is asking them to solve. The blanks in the story will identify the characters involved as well as the numbers. The students will then be asked to show how they solved the problem. They can show their understanding of the problem in pictures, words, and in symbols. You will want to encourage the students to show their thinking in multiple ways.

Management
1. Prior to teaching this lesson make one set of bags for each group by writing *Characters* on one bag and *Numbers* on the other. Cut out the individual characters and place them in the bag labeled *Characters*. The numbers will be placed in the *Numbers* bag. Each group will also need a set of story problems.
2. Students can work in groups of two to four students.
3. In several instances, students will need to place their selected numbers in an order that will avoid the use of negative numbers. They should not glue down any numbers until an order has been determined for them. Optional: If a selected number will not work in a given situation, have students draw another number or make up one of their own.

Procedure
1. Write the following problem on the board and read it with the students.
  Vivian Vole has a collection of 12 pebbles. Foster Frog has collected 38 pebbles. Who has the most pebbles?
2. Ask the students to first identify the problem they are trying to solve. [who has the most pebbles] After the students have identified the problem, underline the sentence that identifies what they are being asked to solve. Ask the students what else they need to know to be able to solve the problem. [who has the pebbles and how many pebbles each one has]

AWESOME ADDITION AND SUPER SUBTRACTION

3. Distribute the brown bags. Have the students read the labels on the bags. Explain to them that these bags contain pictures of characters and numbers.
4. Ask, "Which of these bags would have something you need in order to solve the problem on the board?" [both bags]
5. Ask them how many characters and numbers they need to be able to solve the problem. [two characters and two numbers]
6. Distribute the first student page and tell the students to draw two characters and two numbers from the bag and glue them in the correct locations in the story.
7. Have each group solve the problem and share their answers. Tell them they will need to show their work in numbers, pictures, and/or words. Talk about why there were different answers. [The answer is dependent upon who the characters are and what the numbers are.]
8. Tell the students they will now solve other problems. Distribute the remaining story problems. Instruct students to decide how many characters and numbers they will need by reading the problem. Remind them that they must first underline the problem and then show how they solved the problem using numbers, pictures, and/or words.
9. When all groups have finished, let groups share some of their stories and solutions.

Connecting Learning
1. What is the first step involved in solving a story problem? [Underlining the question you are trying to answer.]
2. How did you decide what went in each blank in the rebus story?
3. What three things do you need to know to be able to solve a story problem? [the question, the characters, and the numbers]
4. How are these three parts related to each other?
5. How did this activity help you become better at solving story problems?

* Reprinted with permission from *Principles and Standards for School Mathematics*, 2000 by the National Council of Teachers of Mathematics. All rights reserved.

Key Question

How can we solve a variety of story problems?

Learning Goals

Students will:

- identify problems to be solved in stories; and

- solve problems using words, pictures, and/or symbols.

Uncle Rebus Stories

_____ has a collection of _____ pebbles.

_____ has collected _____ pebbles. Who has the most pebbles?

Uncle Rebus Stories

Yesterday at the pond, _____ counted _____ dragonflies.

When a bird flew overhead, _____ dragonflies flew away.

How many were left?

Uncle Rebus Stories

_____ and _____ were going on a picnic. They invited _____ to go with them. They ate _____ oranges, _____ apples, and _____ bananas. How many pieces of fruit did they eat?

Uncle Rebus Stories

In _____'s garden there are _____ flowers.

_____ are tulips. The rest are sunflowers.

How many are sunflowers?

Uncle Rebus Stories

It was a very warm day. _____ and _____ sold

_____ glasses of lemonade from their stand in the morning and

_____ glasses of lemonade in the afternoon.

When did they sell the most lemonade?

Uncle Rebus Stories

_____ baked some cookies. _____ baked _____ cookies. They had 80 cookies altogether.

Who baked the most cookies?

Uncle Rebus Stories

———— had 90 nuts and 35 berries. He gave some nuts to ————, his best friend. Now he has ———— left. How many did he give to his best friend?

Uncle Rebus Stories

On a warm spring day _____, _____, and _____ went on a walk. They counted _____ robins, _____ blue birds, and _____ squirrels. How many birds did they count?

Uncle Rebus Stories

_____ and _____ went down to the pond on a sunny fall day. They watched squirrels gather _____ acorns, _____ sunflower seeds, and _____ pumpkin seeds. How many more seeds did the squirrels gather than acorns?

Uncle Rebus Stories

32	14	7	4	12
56	24	17	9	10
19	48	25	38	41
20	35	73	66	2

Connecting Learning

1. What is the first step involved in solving a story problem?

2. How did you decide what went in each blank in the rebus story?

3. What three things do you need to know to be able to solve a story problem?

4. How are these three parts related to each other?

5. How did this activity help you become better at solving story problems?

Sharing and Solving Stories

These stories will give your students practice doing addition and subtraction problems that match situations in their daily lives. Several ideas are given, but you and/or your students can write and solve many more. Students become better problem solvers if they are given multiple opportunities and methods to solve problems. Students need time to talk and share their processes.

In these stories, the students are always first asked to identify the problem for each question. They are then asked to solve the problem and show their work using words, drawings, and/or numbers. The final thing they are asked to do is to be able to explain how they solved the problem.

Example
Today is the second of January. How many days have passed since it was Christmas? (Use this pattern for other holidays and events.)

- Identify the question.
- Solve the problem and show your work in words, drawings, and/or numbers.
- Be prepared to explain how you solved the problem.

The question is how many days have passed since it was Christmas. The students should be able to tell you that it has been eight days since Christmas. They could use a calendar to solve the problem. They can count on from the 25th of December until January 2nd. Whatever method they use, their explanations—written and oral—should reflect how they went about solving the problem. The shared strategies for solving problems should help all your students become better problem solvers.

Today is _____. _____'s birthday is on _____. How many more days until he or she will celebrate it?
(Example: Today is April 5th. Tyrese's birthday is April 18th. How many more days until he will celebrate his birthday?

- Identify the question.
- Solve the problem and show your work in words, drawings, and/or numbers.
- Be prepared to explain how you solved the problem.

Today _____ students are buying their lunches and _____ students brought their lunches. How many more are buying than bringing lunches?

- Identify the question.
- Solve the problem and show your work in words, drawings, and/or numbers.
- Be prepared to explain how you solved the problem.

We went to the book fair yesterday. Keel bought seven books, Amber bought 11 books, and James bought eight books. How many books did the three students buy altogether?

- Identify the question.
- Solve the problem and show your work in words, drawings, and/or numbers.
- Be prepared to explain how you solved the problem.

AWESOME ADDITION AND SUPER SUBTRACTION © 2010 AIMS Education Foundation

Matthew had 25 cents before he went to school. He found some money on the way to school and now he has 87 cents. How much money did he find?

- Identify the question.
- Solve the problem and show your work in words, drawings, and/or numbers.
- Be prepared to explain how you solved the problem.
- What coins could he have found?

Ava and David baked cookies for the school's bake sale. Ava baked 48. They had a total of 84 to sell. How many cookies did David bake?

- Identify the question.
- Solve the problem and show your work in words, drawings, or numbers.
- Be prepared to explain how you solved the problem.

Ethan and Olivia went to the zoo this past weekend. They saw 17 birds, 14 snakes, and 12 lizards. How many more birds did they see than lizards?

- Identify the question.
- Solve the problem and show your work in words, drawings, and/or numbers.
- Be prepared to explain how you solved the problem.

Juan has a collection of 32 stamps. Sarah has 26 stamps in her collection. Sadie has 17 stamps in hers. How many stamps do they have altogether?

- Identify the question.
- Solve the problem and show your work in words, drawings, and/or numbers.
- Be prepared to explain how you solved the problem.

The class library has 100 books. Marla checked out eight and Jeff checked out four. How many books are left in the library?

- Identify the question.
- Solve the problem and show your work in words, drawings, and/or numbers.
- Be prepared to explain how you solved the problem.

AWESOME ADDITION AND SUPER SUBTRACTION

Playful and Intelligent Practice

- **Meaning and understanding must precede practice.**
  Students should be able to provide both physical and mathematical evidence that they understand an arithmetic fact before they are asked to memorize the corresponding symbolic basic fact. Look for this evidence in more than one setting.

- **Students should begin to memorize basic arithmetic facts soon after they demonstrate an understanding of symbolic statements.**
  Use concrete materials then move to pictures and models in the initial stages of instruction. There comes a time when a student is expected to use symbols (written numerals) to represent the mathematical ideas and basic facts.

- **Students need daily practice.**
  It is not uncommon to see students hurry through a drill session by figuring out answers. They rapidly count on their fingers or quickly make tally marks and count. These students are not practicing remembering basic facts, they are practicing finger counting or tallying, and they become very good at these procedures. However, the purpose of the playful and intelligent practice is to commit the basic facts to memory and to work toward this goal, not to use other counting methods to remember the answers.

  During practice sessions, do not take time to work out or explain answers. The students should have this understanding before beginning the session.

  Keep the practice session short—five to 10 minutes. Two or three five-minute practice sessions a day will enable children to memorize basic facts.

  Try to focus on only a few basic facts in a given lesson, and always review previously memorized facts. Generally, three or four new facts are a challenge that most students will accept. Even after mastery is attained, review should be continued throughout the primary grades.

  Vary the activities using games, flash cards, oral practice, story telling with storyboards, and more. Keep the sessions enthusiastic and interesting. Praise students for good effort and keep records of their progress.

- **Use tables and charts to introduce students to patterns in the numeration system.**

—Larry Ecklund

Cornering the Facts

Topic
Basic addition/subtraction facts

Key Question
How can a triangle help you learn your basic addition and subtraction facts?

Learning Goals
Students will:
• read an addition/subtraction chart,
• become aware of the commutative property for addition,
• recognize that it does not exist for subtraction, and
• create a personal set of addition and subtraction cards for facts they need to memorize.

Guiding Document
NCTM Standards 2000*
• *Develop and use strategies for whole number computations, with a focus on addition and subtraction*
• *Develop fluency with basic number combinations for addition and subtraction*

Math
Number and operations
    addition
    subtraction

Integrated Processes
Observing
Recording
Comparing and contrasting
Communicating
Applying

Materials
For each student:
    index cards (see *Management 1*)
    Addition/Subtraction Facts Table
    scissors
    Corner Tool (see *Management 2*)

Background Information
There are 100 basic facts for addition and 100 for subtraction. The focus of this activity is to give students a concrete way to see the relationship between addition and subtraction and to focus on the basic facts they do not know. They will construct a tool that will help them learn their basic facts. The students will use this tool to help them develop a better understanding of the commutative property of addition (The Commutative Property of Addition: two whole numbers can be added in either order, a + b or b + a.) as well as the realization that there is not a commutative property for subtraction.

Management
1. The students will need one 5" x 8" index card for every two triangle cards they construct. It is suggested that students only construct cards for the facts on which they need to work.
2. Copy the *Corner Tool* page onto card stock. Each corner tool is made with two strips that are taped or glued together at right angles. Copy the *Transparency Templates* on transprency film. Cut the squares apart. Tape the transparent piece to the back of the *Corner Tool* as illustrated.

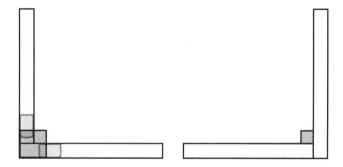

Procedure
1. Distribute the *Addition/Subtraction Facts Table.*
2. Guide the students in searching for patterns in the table. Help them see that it has a line of symmetry that runs diagonally from the upper left to bottom right corners.
3. Discuss with the students some of the patterns they discovered.

AWESOME ADDITION AND SUPER SUBTRACTION   © 2010 AIMS Education Foundation

4. Distribute the assembled *Corner Tools*. Demonstrate how to use the tool to find the addition facts. Ask the students, "Where is the sum (answer) for an addition problem always located?" [It is always located in the corner.]

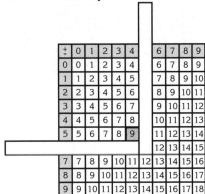

5. Demonstrate how to use the tool to find subtraction facts by placing the transparent piece over the minuend and one arm below (or to the right of) the subtrahend. Ask the students where the difference (the answer) for a subtraction problem is. [It is located at one of the ends of the corner tool.] Ask the students how this is different from addition facts. Help the students see that the order for addition does not matter, but the order for subtraction does matter. Relate this to the commutative property of addition.

6. Direct each student to locate a fact on the *Addition/Subtraction Facts Table* they are having difficulty learning.

7. Distribute the index cards and scissors. Demonstrate how to cut the card to create two triangles.

8. Direct them to record the digit next to the corner of the *Corner Tool* in the corner of the index card that forms the right angle. Have them record the numbers that are at the end of each arm of the *Corner Tool* in each of the other two angles of the card.

9. Ask the students to create cards for each fact with which they are having difficulty.

Connecting Learning
1. How are addition and subtraction related?
2. How do the triangle flashcards help you learn your facts faster?
3. What does the commutative property of addition mean? [The order in which you add the numbers isn't important. Adding 5 and 8 is the same as adding 8 and 5.]
4. Why doesn't the commutative property apply to subtraction? [The order matters. Taking 5 from 8 is not the same as taking 8 from 5.]
5. Why is it important to know your basic addition and subtraction facts?

* Reprinted with permission from *Principles and Standards for School Mathematics,* 2000 by the National Council of Teachers of Mathematics. All rights reserved.

Cornering the Facts

Key Question

How can a triangle help you learn your basic addition and subtraction facts?

Learning Goals

Students will:

- read an addition/subtraction chart,
- become aware of the commutative property for addition,
- recognize that it does not exist for subtraction, and
- create a personal set of addition and subtraction cards for facts they need to memorize.

CORNERING the FACTS Transparency Templates

CORNERING the FACTS — Corner Tools

100 Addition/Subtraction Facts Table

±	0	1	2	3	4	5	6	7	8	9
0	0	1	2	3	4	5	6	7	8	9
1	1	2	3	4	5	6	7	8	9	10
2	2	3	4	5	6	7	8	9	10	11
3	3	4	5	6	7	8	9	10	11	12
4	4	5	6	7	8	9	10	11	12	13
5	5	6	7	8	9	10	11	12	13	14
6	6	7	8	9	10	11	12	13	14	15
7	7	8	9	10	11	12	13	14	15	16
8	8	9	10	11	12	13	14	15	16	17
9	9	10	11	12	13	14	15	16	17	18

Connecting Learning

1. How are addition and subtraction related?

2. How do the triangle flashcards help you learn your facts faster?

3. What does the commutative property of addition mean?

4. Why doesn't the commutative property apply to subtraction?

5. Why is it important to know your basic addition and subtraction facts?

Saluting Subtraction and Addition

Topic
Addition/Subtraction

Key Question
What is the number on your card?

Learning Goal
Students will play a game in which they practice both addition and subtraction as they try to determine either the sum of two cards or the value of a card based on the sum.

Guiding Documents
Project 2061 Benchmark
- Readily give the sums and differences of single-digit numbers in familiar contexts where the operation makes sense to them and they can judge the reasonableness of the answer.

NCTM Standards 2000*
- Develop and use strategies for whole-number computations, with a focus on addition and subtraction
- Develop fluency with basic number combinations for addition and subtraction
- Model situations that involve the addition and subtraction of whole numbers, using objects, pictures, and symbols
- Build new mathematical knowledge through problem solving

Math
Number and operations
    addition
    subtraction
    equations
Problem solving
Algerbraic thinking

Integrated Processes
Observing
Inferring
Applying

Materials
Playing cards (see *Management 1*)
Recording pages

Background Information
In this activity, a game gives students playful, intelligent practice with their addition and subtraction facts while working on their problem-solving skills. One student is the "general" and the other two are "soldiers." When the general calls, "Salute," the soldiers raise a card to their heads. The general quickly gives the sum of the two cards, and the soldiers compete to determine the values of their cards by looking at what the other player has. The roles rotate so that each student gets practice both with subtraction and addition facts for the numbers from one to 10.

In addition to practicing fluency with addition and subtraction facts, students will be challenged to record the equations that represent each round of play. For each round, three (or four) different equations will be written, depending on the perspective of the student. This allows them to see the relationships between the fact families ($5 + 1 = 6$, $6 - 5 = 1$, $6 - 1 = 5$).

Management
1. Each group of three students needs a deck of playing cards with the face cards (jack, queen, king) and jokers removed. If playing cards are not available, you can make cards by writing numbers on 3" x 5" index cards or card stock sheets cut into eighths. Depending on the ages and abilities of your students, you may wish to further restrict the scope of the activity by removing some of the higher number cards.
2. There are two parts to this game. *Part One* is played by three players, and *Part Two* is played by four players. If necessary, additional students can be in a group with a different player sitting out each round. This will require additional games to be played so that each student gets equal participation (two games as a soldier and one game as the general).
3. Students will need one or two copies of each recording page. Once they are comfortable with the process for recording, they can keep track of the equations and points on scratch paper.

AWESOME ADDITION AND SUPER SUBTRACTION   131   © 2010 AIMS Education Foundation

Procedure
1. Invite two students to come to the front of the class to help you demonstrate the game. Give each student half of the deck of cards (see *Management 1*). Instruct them to hold the cards in a stack, face down.
2. Explain that you are the general and they are the soldiers. When you say, "Salute," they are to take the top card from the stack and raise it to their foreheads so that both the other player and you can see it. You will tell them the sum of the two cards displayed. The first one of them to correctly identify the card he or she is holding gets a point. Be sure students understand that an ace is equal to one.
3. Have the class identify the process that will be needed for the soldiers to determine the values of cards they are holding. [subtract the number on the other player's card from the sum]
4. Call, "Salute" and have the students raise the cards to their foreheads and try to determine what they are. Once a player is successful, have group members look at their cards to verify that they are correct.
5. As a class, determine the equations (number sentences) that can be represented using the cards and record them on the board. Identify which equation corresponds to which student. For example, if the two cards flipped are a 4 and a 9, the equations would be: $4 + 9 = 13$ or $9 + 4 = 13$ (general), $13 - 4 = 9$ (soldier one), and $13 - 9 = 4$ (soldier two). Discuss how there are two possible equations for the general.
6. Repeat this several times so that the class gets used to the process. Be sure that the students know to put the cards that have been flipped over in a pile to the side.
7. Once students understand the procedure for the game, divide them into groups of three. Give each group a deck of cards. Give each student a recording page on which to keep track of the points and the equations for each round. Point out that there is only space for the general to record one equation each round, and explain that it doesn't matter which one is written down.
8. Explain that one game has three rounds. After each game, the cards are shuffled and divided into two equal stacks. Also, the roles switch and a different player gets to be the general.
9. Allow time for students to play the game until each student has been the general once and a soldier twice.

Part Two
1. Divide students into groups of four. Explain that this time, there are three soldiers instead of two. The goal will be the same, but the challenge will be more difficult.
2. Instruct students to remove all of the cards from six to 10 so that only ace through five remain in the deck. Have them mix the deck and divide it into three piles.
3. Distribute the student page for *Part Two* and remind students that they will be responsible for writing the equations for each round of play.
4. Allow time for groups to play the game until everyone has had the chance to be a soldier three times and the general once.
5. Discuss the differences between the two games and what students learned. Encourage students to think of variations of the game that they can try.

Connecting Learning
1. As a soldier, what did you have to do to determine the value on your card in *Part One*? [subtract the number on the other player's card from the sum]
2. Was it easier for you to be the general or one of the soldiers? Why?
3. How did the game change in *Part Two*?
4. Was it more or less difficult with three soldiers? Explain.
5. As a soldier, what did you have to do to determine the value of your card in *Part Two*? [subtract the numbers on the other two soldiers' cards from the sum given by the general]
6. How did you determine the equation to write down each turn?
7. How was your equation like the ones for the other members of your group? [uses the same numbers] How was it different? [different numbers in different places, addition instead of subtraction, etc.]
8. What variations of the game can you think of to try?

Extension
Have students think of variations on the game and try them.

* Reprinted with permission from *Principles and Standards for School Mathematics*, 2000 by the National Council of Teachers of Mathematics. All rights reserved.

Saluting Subtraction and Addition

Key Question

What is the number on your card?

Learning Goal

Students will:

play a game in which they practice both addition and subtraction as they try to determine either the sum of two cards or the value of a card based on the sum.

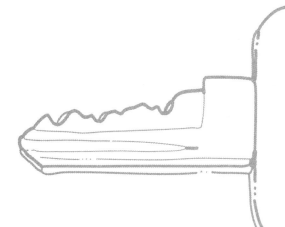

Saluting Subtraction and Addition
Part One

Record your equations for each round. Keep track of points.

Round One Equations

General: _____ + _____ = _____

Soldier One: _____ − _____ = _____

Soldier Two: _____ − _____ = _____

Round Two Equations

General: _____ + _____ = _____

Soldier One: _____ − _____ = _____

Soldier Two: _____ − _____ = _____

Round Three Equations

General: _____ + _____ = _____

Soldier One: _____ − _____ = _____

Soldier Two: _____ − _____ = _____

Points

_____ Soldier One

_____ Soldier Two

AWESOME ADDITION AND SUPER SUBTRACTION © 2010 AIMS Education Foundation

Part Two

Record one of your equations for each round. Keep track of points.

Round One Equations

G: _____ + _____ + _____ = _____   S1: _____ − _____ − _____ = _____

S2: _____ − _____ − _____ = _____   S3: _____ − _____ − _____ = _____

Round Two Equations

G: _____ + _____ + _____ = _____   S1: _____ − _____ − _____ = _____

S2: _____ − _____ − _____ = _____   S3: _____ − _____ − _____ = _____

Round Three Equations

G: _____ + _____ + _____ = _____   S1: _____ − _____ − _____ = _____

S2: _____ − _____ − _____ = _____   S3: _____ − _____ − _____ = _____

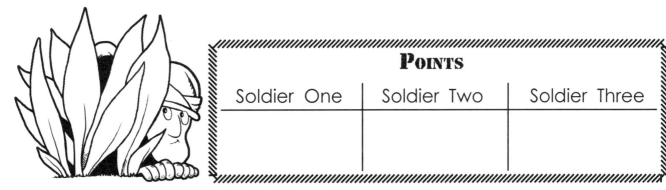

Points		
Soldier One	Soldier Two	Soldier Three

AWESOME ADDITION AND SUPER SUBTRACTION

Connecting Learning

1. As a soldier, what did you have to do to determine the value on your card in *Part One?*

2. Was it easier for you to be the general or one of the soldiers? Why?

3. How did the game change in *Part Two?*

4. Was it more or less difficult with three soldiers? Explain.

Connecting Learning

5. As a soldier, what did you have to do to determine the value of your card in *Part Two?*

6. How did you determine the equation to write down each turn?

7. How was your equation like the ones for the other members of your group? How was it different?

8. What variations of the game can you think of to try?

Hands on the Addition and Subtraction Table

Purpose of the Game
Students will explore the addition and subtraction table.

Materials
For each group of four students:
  50 index cards, 3" x 5"
  4 colored markers (see *Management 1*)
  scissors
  addition and subtraction table

Management
1. Each member in a group needs to use the same color marker.
2. The students will need to place a line under the number 9 so that it can be distinguished from the number 6.

Directions
Part One
1. Direct the students to cut the addition and subtraction table along the bold lines. This will divide the table into four equal parts.
2. Tell each student to select one of the four sections of the table that has been cut apart.
3. Demonstrate how to fold one of the index cards in half and cut it apart. Tell students that they will need to fold and cut the 50 cards that their group was given.
4. After each group has cut the cards, tell them to divide them equally within their group.
5. Direct each student to copy the numbers from the section of the addition/subtraction table they have onto the index cards they prepared. Show them how to draw a line under any nine so that the students will be able to distinguish the difference between it and a six.

Part Two
1. Tell the students the object of the game is to build the addition and subtraction table.
2. Direct one student in each group to shuffle and deal the cards to the students in the group. Each student will have 25 cards.
3. Play begins with the student on the left of the dealer. He or she may place any card on the table.
4. Play continues clockwise around the table. The student may only play a card that will touch the card played on the table. The card may share an edge or a diagonal corner. If there are no plays, the student skips a turn and play continues clockwise.

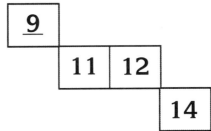

5. The winner is the one who is able to play all of his or her cards first.
6. After the students have completely constructed the addition and subtraction table, discuss strategies they used as well as patterns they discovered.

AWESOME ADDITION AND SUPER SUBTRACTION

Hands on the Addition and Subtraction Table

0	1	2	3	4	5	6	7	8	9
1	2	3	4	5	6	7	8	9	10
2	3	4	5	6	7	8	9	10	11
3	4	5	6	7	8	9	10	11	12
4	5	6	7	8	9	10	11	12	13
5	6	7	8	9	10	11	12	13	14
6	7	8	9	10	11	12	13	14	15
7	8	9	10	11	12	13	14	15	16
8	9	10	11	12	13	14	15	16	17
9	10	11	12	13	14	15	16	17	18

AWESOME ADDITION AND SUPER SUBTRACTION © 2010 AIMS Education Foundation

Make It Even

Purpose of the Game
Students will play a card game that challenges them to use mental math to find equations that equal even sums between 10 and 18.

Materials
Make It Even cards, one set per student

Management
1. This game can be played with even target sums ranging from 10 to 18. (Games can also be played with target sums lower than 10, but the smaller the sum, the fewer the cards and the shorter the game.)
2. Each student will need a set of *Make It Even* cards. These cards should be copied onto card stock and laminated for durability. These cards can also be ordered from AIMS, (item number 4158).
3. The target sum will determine the cards that students need to use. Look at the table below to help you determine which cards to use with your students. *Note: When using card sets that begin with 1, 1, no cards with a zero can be in the set, even if they have a sum that is greater than 1, 1. Likewise, no cards containing a 7, 8, or 9 may be used in a set that ends with 6, 6, even if their sum is less than 6, 6.*

Target Sum	Cards
18	All
16	0,0 to 8,8 or 1,1 to 7,7
14	0,0 to 7,7 or 1,1 to 6,6 or 2,2 to 9,9
12	0,0 to 6,6 or 1,1 to 5,5
10	0,0 to 5,5

Directions
1. Have students shuffle their *Make It Even* cards and lay them face up on the desk, in stacks of two. There should always be one extra card, which can be placed on any of the stacks. For example, if students were playing with the cards 0, 0 to 5, 5 (target sum = 10), they would have 10 stacks, as shown below.

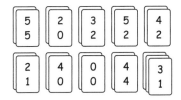

2. The object is to match cards that total the target sum. For example, with the illustrated cards, the 5, 5 and the 0, 0 are a pair; the 4, 2 and the 4, 0 are a pair; the 5, 2 and the 2, 1 are a pair, and so on. When students see a pair of cards that totals the target sum, those two cards are removed from the stacks and set aside.
3. Students continue to pair and remove cards until only one card is left. If students should get to a place where none of the visible cards pair up to total the target sum, they may move the top card from one stack into any empty space.
4. If students have correctly paired the cards, the one remaining card will always be one-half the target sum. For example, if the target sum is 16, the final card will have a sum of eight. If the target sum is 10, the final card will have a sum of five, and so on.
5. Once students have had a chance to play the game several times, add the additional challenge of time. Play "Beat the Clock," and have students race to see if they can finish the game within a set amount of time.

Variation
A two-person version of this game can be played in a more competitive format. In pairs, have students shuffle one set of *Make It Even* cards and lay out nine cards, face up, in three rows of three. As students see two cards that add up to the target sum, they call out "Sum." They then remove the two cards that they saw, stating the addition problem out loud. If the target sum is 14, a student might say, "Five and five is 10, three and one is four, 10 and four is 14." The removed cards are replaced by two more from the deck, and the game continues until all of the cards have been dealt and the pairs have been made. The player with the most pairs at the end of the game is the winner.

Extension
Experiment with different sets of cards for the various target sums (e.g., use 0, 0 to 7, 7 for a target sum of 14; or 0, 0 to 6, 6 for a target sum of 12). Which sets can you get to work? Are they still self-checking? Why or why not?

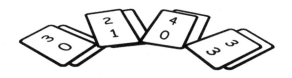

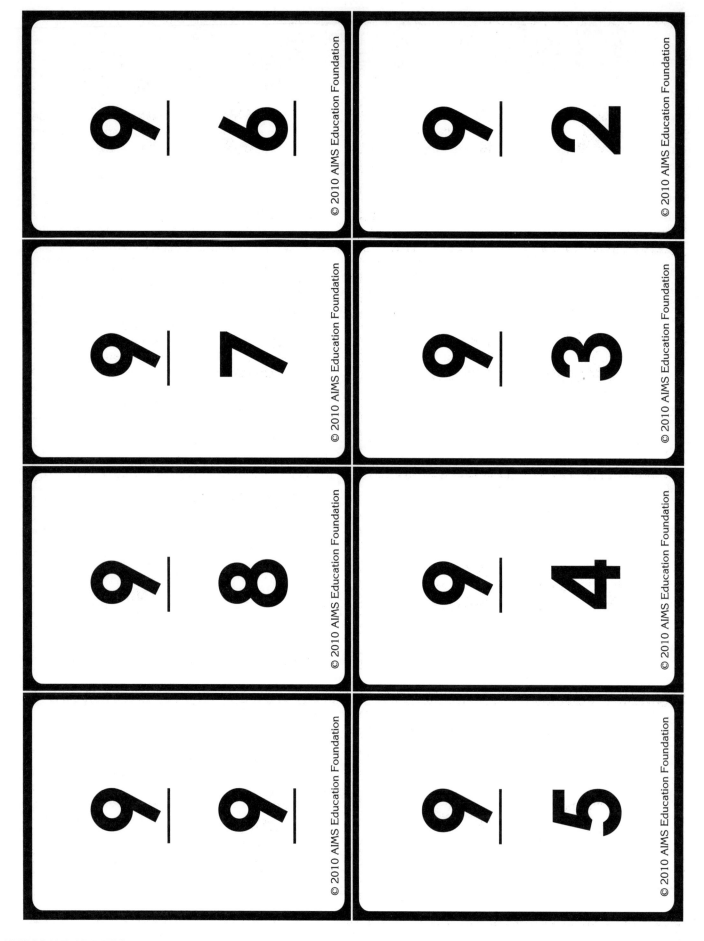

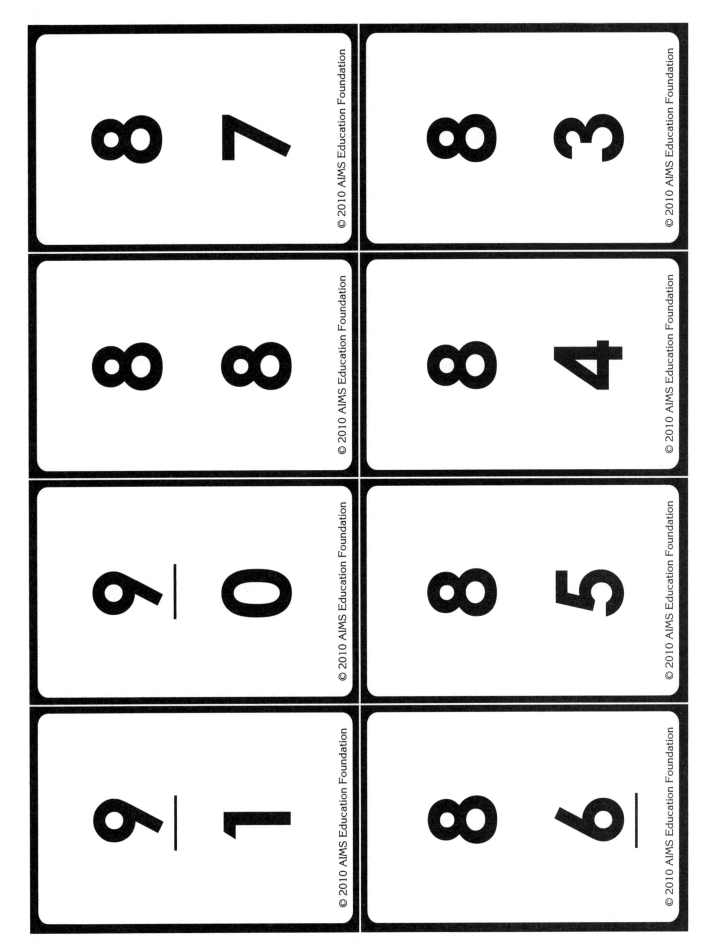

7 - 7	7 - 3
8 - 0	7 - 4
8 - 1	7 - 5
8 - 2	7 - 6

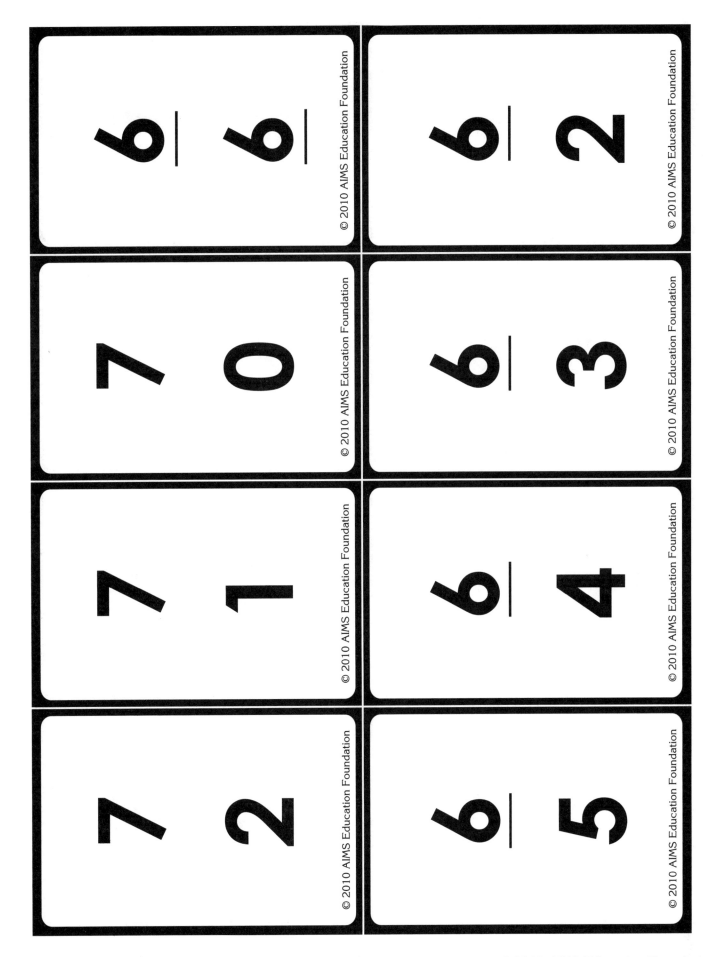

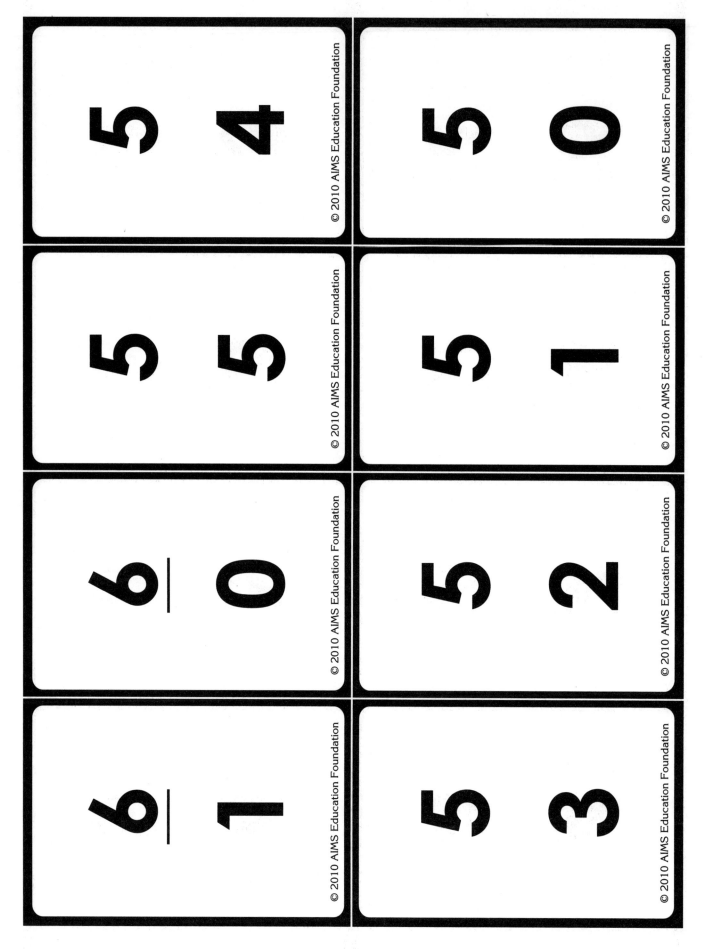

4	3
1	1

4	3
2	2

4	3
3	3

4	4
4	0

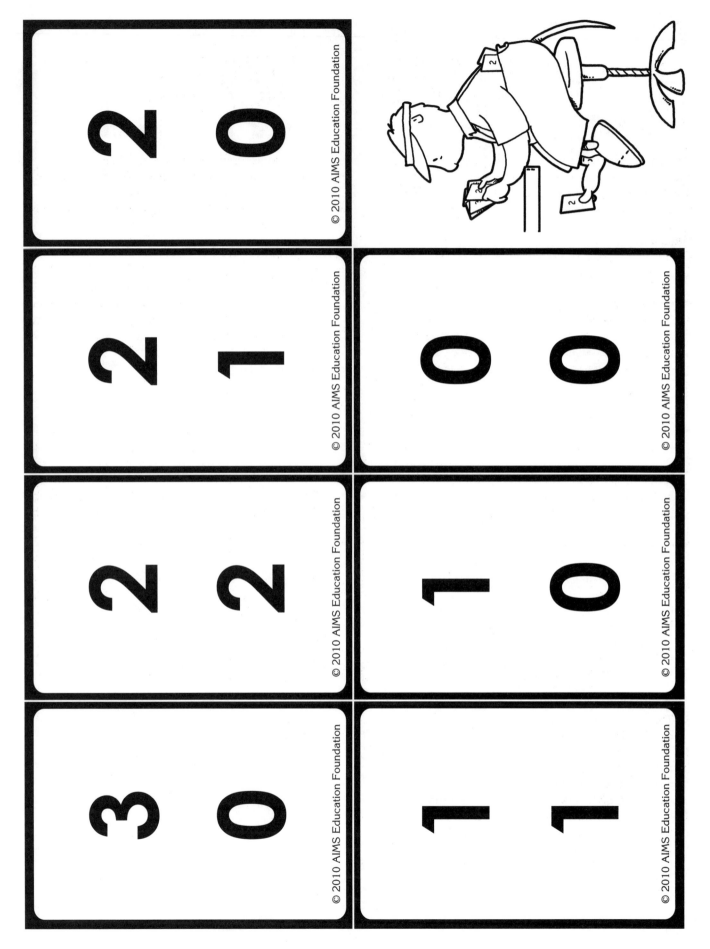

Roll Play

Purpose of the Game
Students will experience some playful, intelligent practice for addition facts, subtraction facts, number sense, and place value.

Materials
Colored dice (see *Management 2*)
Counters (see *Management 3*)

Management
1. These games are well suited for centers or other small-group settings when a few students are playing them at a time. This also reduces the amount of materials necessary. Students must play in pairs.
2. To play the games, each student will need two dice. One player's dice must be a different color from the other's to keep them visually separated. You may also want to provide students with box lids to roll the dice in so that they don't go off the table.
3. Players will need five to 10 beans, buttons, or other similar objects each. The number of objects will determine the length of each game, so give students fewer objects for shorter games.

Addition Roll Play
Directions
1. Both players roll their dice at the same time and, as quickly as possible, say the sum of the two numbers rolled. If a player is unable to say his or her sum within a few seconds, he or she forfeits one counter to the other player. (You will have to determine what is a reasonable amount of time to allow. Students should have a few seconds to think, but not enough time to count the sum on their fingers.)
2. The player who has a higher sum collects one counter from the other player.
3. When both players roll the same sum, a war commences. Each player leaves the die with the higher number and rolls the second die again. The player with the higher new sum is the winner and receives two counters from the losing player. Should there be a second tie, the process is repeated until one player has a higher sum. The number of counters collected by the winner is equivalent to the number of rolls. (If keeping track of the number of rolls is too difficult for your students, you may choose to assign a fixed number of counters to be collected after a war, regardless of the number of rolls it takes to determine a winner.)
4. Play continues until one player has accumulated all of the counters.

Subtraction Roll Play
Directions
1. Play like *Addition Roll Play*, but instead of adding the numbers rolled, subtract the smaller number from the larger number. The player with the *lower* difference wins.

Double-Digit Roll Play
Directions
1. Instead of adding or subtracting the numbers rolled, combine them to make two-digit numbers. Whichever number is called out first is the one that must be used, even if it is the lower of the two possibilities. For example, if a student rolls a four and a six and says "46," that is the value that will be compared to the other player's roll, even though it would have been possible to have a "64" with those two numbers.

Variations
1. Give each player three or four dice instead of two.
2. Increase the number of players to three. In the event of a three-way war, all players continue to roll as long as there is a tie. As soon as one player loses, he or she ceases to roll. Each player contributes the number of counters equivalent to the number of times he or she rolled.

Seek and Hide

Purpose of the Game
Students will gain practice with basic addition facts by adding the totals from rolling a pair of dice and covering those sums on a game board in an attempt to be the first to cover an entire row or column.

Materials
For each pair of students:
   game board (sums to 12)
   two dice
   20 colored chips per player (see *Management 2*)

Management
1. Both versions of the activity are meant to be played in pairs. In *Version One*, each student needs his or her own game board. In *Version Two*, players share a single board.
2. In order to play *Version Two* of this game, each student will need a different color of chips so that a distinction can be made between the players' pieces.

Directions
Version One
1. Roll both dice. Find the sum of the numbers rolled.
2. Cover a single space on your game board that is equivalent to the sum of the numbers rolled. If no spaces with that sum are available, your turn is over.
3. Alternate rolling the dice until one player has covered an entire horizontal or vertical row on his or her game board.

Version Two
1. Roll both dice. Find the sum of the numbers rolled.
2. Using chips in your color, cover a single space on the game board that is equivalent to the sum of the numbers rolled. The challenge is not only to cover an entire row, but also to prevent the other player from doing so. If no spaces with that sum are available, your turn is over.
3. Alternate rolling the dice until one player has covered an entire horizontal or vertical row on the shared game board with chips of his or her color.

Variations
1. Play until the entire board is covered.
2. Make the challenge to cover diagonals, corners, a 3 x 3 block of numbers, etc.
3. Use three dice instead of two. This version requires using the game board that has values from three to 18.
4. In *Version Two*, allow students to either play a chip of their own on any space with the sum they rolled, or remove one of the other player's chips from a space with that sum.

Seek and Hide

Sums to 12

Use with two dice.

7	9	4	12	3	7
2	8	6	9	5	11
10	3	7	6	8	2
6	11	5	7	4	9
4	5	8	2	6	10
6	7	10	3	12	4
12	9	5	2	7	8

AWESOME ADDITION AND SUPER SUBTRACTION © 2010 AIMS Education Foundation

Seek and Hide

Sums to 18

Use with three dice.

7	9	4	12	10	15
14	3	13	18	8	11
10	16	11	6	13	9
5	11	9	12	15	7
16	6	8	14	5	10
9	13	10	15	12	6
12	14	7	11	17	8

Spin to Win

Purpose of the Game
Students will practice their addition and subtraction facts in the context of a game.

Materials
For each group:
  spinner (see *Management 2*)
  paper lunch sack (see *Management 3*)
  10 Teddy Bear Counters—five yellow and five green
  student page (for every two students)

Management
1. This game is designed to be played in pairs or groups of no more than four.
2. To make the spinner, cut out the arrow and color it half yellow and half green as indicated. Attach the arrow to the center of the circle using a paper fastener. Another method is to mount the circle on corrugated cardboard and attach the arrow with a pushpin or thumbtack. Whichever method you use, be sure that the arrow spins freely.
3. Fill a paper lunch sack or similar opaque bag with 10 Teddy Bear Counters—five yellow and five green. If you do not have Teddy Bear Counters, you may use other objects instead, as long as they are uniform and of two different colors—green and yellow.
4. This game may be played in a whole-class session, or you may choose to have it at a center where students can play it repeatedly throughout the week for short periods of time.
5. There are enough spaces in the recording tables for each student to record 10 spins. Depending on the ages and abilities of your students, you may want to increase or decrease the number of spins in one game.

Rules
1. Spin the spinner. If it lands on a line, spin it again until it is in a space.
2. Draw a bear from the bag.
3. If the bear is yellow, look at the yellow end of the spinner. *Add* the two numbers in the spaces on either side of the arrow.
4. If the bear is green, look at the green end of the spinner. *Find the difference* between the two numbers in the spaces on either side of the arrow.
5. Record the sum or difference in the table.
6. Put the bear back in the bag.
7. After all players have had 10 spins, add up the scores for each spin. The player with the highest total score is the winner.
8. If two players have the same total, spin one more time to break the tie.

AWESOME ADDITION AND SUPER SUBTRACTION

Spin to Win

Name:_____   Name:_____

Spin	Total
1	
2	
3	
4	
5	
6	
7	
8	
9	
10	
Grand Total	

Spin	Total
1	
2	
3	
4	
5	
6	
7	
8	
9	
10	
Grand Total	

Fact Finding

Purpose of the Game
Students will complete equations by filling in the missing numbers.

Materials
Playing cards (see *Management 2*)
Scratch paper
Pencils

Management
1. This game can be played with two to four players.
2. Each group of students needs the one (ace) through 10 in all four suits from a deck of cards.

Directions
1. Write seven number sentences, each missing one number. The missing numbers can be any number one through 10. For example, 3 + ___ = 12, ___ – 5 = 4, 2 + ___ = 10, etc.
2. Give the number sentences to another player.
3. Shuffle the deck of cards and place it in the center of the table. Take turns flipping over the top card from the deck.
4. If the card flipped can be used to complete one of that player's number sentences, that card is kept and another card is turned over. If the card cannot be used, it is discarded and that player's turn is over.
5. The first player to complete all of his/her number sentences is the winner.

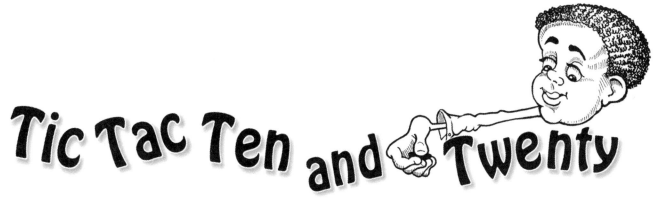

Tic Tac Ten and Twenty

Purpose of the Game
Students will practice basic subtraction facts with numbers between one and 20.

Materials
For each set of partners:
  one *Tic Tac Ten* or *Tic Tac Twenty* spinner (see *Management 1*)
  two game cards
  18 marking chips, nine each of two colors

Management
1. There are two versions of this game, one that has students subtract numbers from 10, and one that has students subtract numbers from 11-20. Choose the most appropriate version for your students and use the appropriate spinner. The game cards remain the same for both versions.
2. This game is designed to be played in pairs. Each pair needs the appropriate spinner, two game cards, and 18 marking chips, nine each of two colors.
3. One easy way to make the spinners is by holding a paper clip in place with a sharpened pencil.
4. Cut apart the game cards before they are given to students so that each child can have one. Each of the four cards on the page is different, so be sure that partners do not have the same game card. Have students play several rounds of the game, using different cards each time.

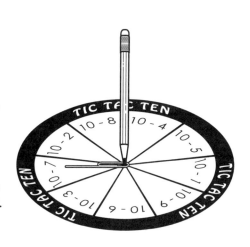

Directions
1. One student begins by spinning the spinner and solving the subtraction problem on which the spinner stops. Students should say the problem out loud, "Ten minus eight is two." If they are correct, they place a marking chip on the space that has that answer on their game card.
2. The second player spins the spinner and repeats this process, using marking chips of a different color.
3. If a player spins a problem for which the solution is already covered, his/her turn is over, and the other player gets to spin.
4. The game is over when one player gets three marking chips in a row horizontally, vertically, or diagonally.

Variations
1. Offer other challenges by making the object of the game to cover the four corners, or diagonals only.
2. Allow both students to place a chip on their boards each time the spinner is spun.
3. Have students both play on the same board. In this case, games may end in a tie when it is not possible for either player to get three chips in a row.
4. When playing on the same board, allow students to remove their opponent's markers as well as place their own. For example, if a student spun a 10 – 2, and the 8 space was already occupied by the other player, he or she could choose to remove that chip. The next time he or she spun a 10 – 2, he or she could fill the space with his or her own chip.

Tic Tac Ten and Twenty

Tic Tac Twenty Spinner

Tic Tac Ten and Twenty Game Cards

Rally With Differences

Purpose of the Game
Students will practice recalling the basic subtraction facts from 10 and/or 20.

Materials
For each group of students:
 one *Rally With Differences* game board
 a place marker for each player in a different color

Management
1. There are two versions of this game, one that has students subtract numbers from 10, and one that has them subtract numbers from 20. Choose the version that is most appropriate for your students and give them the corresponding game board.
2. Copy the game boards onto card stock and laminate for durability. Make each spinner by attaching a small paper clip to the center with a paper fastener.
3. Students should play in groups of three or four.

Directions
1. All markers begin on the space marked "Start." Players spin to see who goes first. Highest spin begins.
2. The first player spins the spinner and subtracts that number from 10 (or 20). Students should say the problem out loud, "Twenty minus 16 is four."
3. If they are correct, students move their markers that number of spaces. If they are incorrect, they forfeit their turn.
4. Play continues in a clockwise direction, with each player spinning the spinner, saying the subtraction problem, and moving their marker the correct number of spaces.
5. The game is over when one player reaches the "Finish" space.

Variation
Instead of moving the markers ahead the number of spaces indicated by the difference, each player simply moves ahead one space if he or she gives the correct response. If a player does not give the correct response, the marker is not moved on the board, and the turn goes to the next player. A time limit may need to be set on responses in this variation.

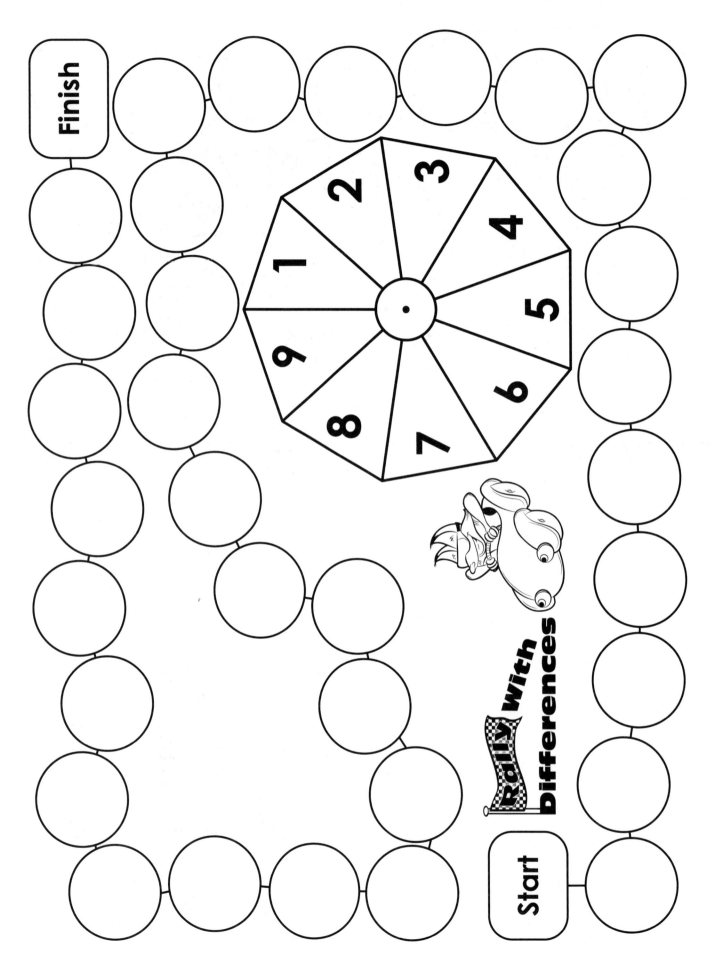

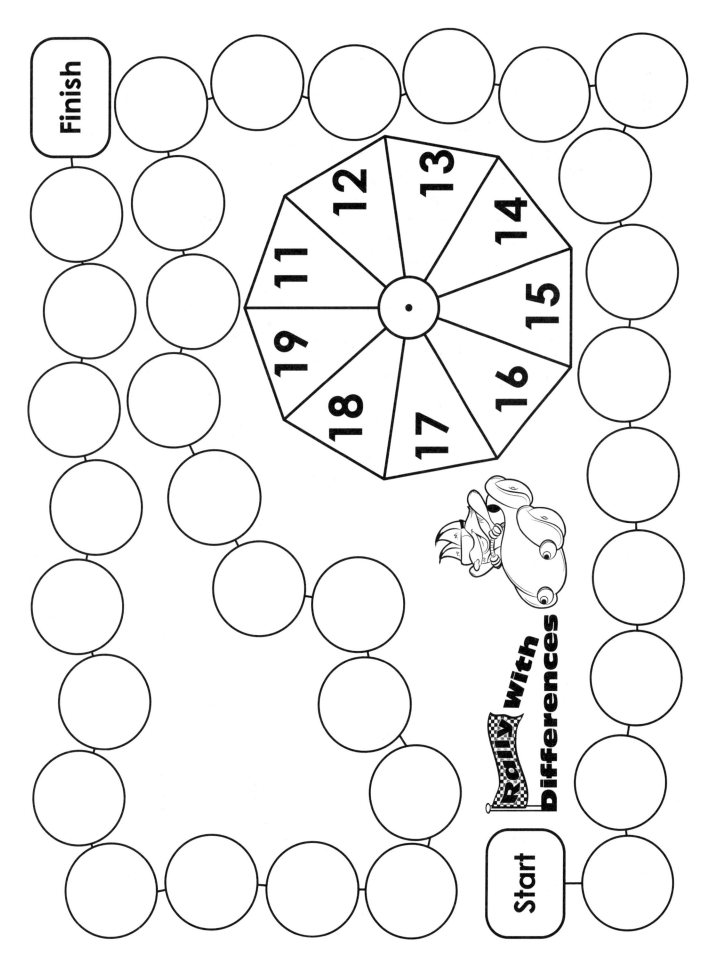

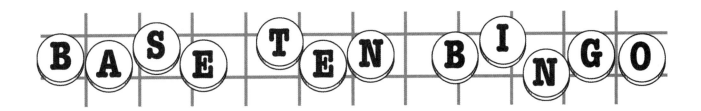

Topic
Place value

Key Question
Why is it important to recognize numbers in a variety of formats?

Learning Goals
Students will:
- build, read, and write numbers; and
- gain practice in identifying numbers written in expanded notation, as words, and as picture representations.

Guiding Document
NCTM Standards 2000*
- *Use multiple models to develop initial understandings of place value and the base-ten number system*
- *Develop a sense of whole numbers and represent and use them in flexible ways, including relating, composing, and decomposing numbers*
- *Connect number words and numerals to the quantities they represent, using various physical models and representations*

Math
Number sense
  place value

Materials
For the class:
  clue cards (see *Management 1*)
  Base Ten Blocks (see *Management 2*)

For each student:
  game board (see *Management 3*)
  covering markers (see *Management 4*)

Background Information
The Base Ten Blocks used in this activity show a proportional relationship. The longs are ten times larger than the units, and the flats are ten times larger than the longs. When the students have grasped the understanding of the relationship, they are asked to use the blocks to model their understanding of place value and the base-ten system.

This activity provides an opportunity for the students to use the Base Ten Blocks to develop an understanding of the value of the place as well as the value of the face of the digits by building, reading and writing large numbers.

Management
1. Plan to display the clue cards using a projection device.
2. One set of Base Ten Blocks is needed for each group of four students. Base Ten Blocks are available from AIMS (item number 4008).
3. Three game cards have been provided for you so that all students do not get a "bingo" at the same time. Copy one card per student onto card stock and laminate for extended use.
4. Each child will need 20 markers to cover the numbers on their game boards. Beans, colored bingo chips, or small squares of paper all work well.

Procedures
Part One
1. Show the class one unit Base Ten Block and ask the students to identify what it represents. [one]
2. Display a Base Ten long and ask the students to identify what it represents. When the class identifies it as a "ten," ask them to prove that it is a "ten." Discuss possible ways to prove that it is a ten. Repeat this process using the flat of one hundred.
3. When the class is comfortable with the manipulative, build a number using the Base Ten Blocks and ask someone to identify the number. Ask another child to come to the board and write the number. Draw a line before and after the number and ask a third child to write the numbers that would come before and after the number on the number line. Repeat this process several times.
4. Once the students are able to identify numbers when they are modeled using the Base Ten Blocks, tell them that you will now write the numbers and that you would like them to use the Base Ten Blocks to build the numbers.
5. Write a number on the board and have the students build the number. Invite a student to model the number using Base Ten Blocks. Discuss how many tens and how many ones they have. Demonstrate how

AWESOME ADDITION AND SUPER SUBTRACTION © 2010 AIMS Education Foundation

this number can also be written in expanded notation. For example, 73 is seven tens + three ones. Repeat this process several times. Discuss which way the students prefer to represent numbers.

Part Two
1. Distribute a game board and covering markers to each child.
2. Explain to the class that they will be playing a game as a review of place value and the first student to cover a complete row, column, or diagonal should call out "bingo."
3. Tell the class that you will display a clue card and they will need to read the clue and cover only one number that is a correct response to the clue. Tell students that in many cases, there will be more than one correct answer.
4. Display the first clue and allow time for the students to cover an appropriate number on their game boards. When displaying the free card, inform the students that they may cover any empty space. Continue displaying the clue cards one at a time until a student says "bingo." When a bingo is called, have that student identify which numbers he or she has covered in a row, column, or diagonal. Compare the winner's numbers to the cards that have been displayed to determine if the student has won the game.
5. Play the game several times and discuss which representation the students think is easiest to read and understand.

Connecting Learning
1. Which way would you prefer to write numbers? Why?
2. Which way would you prefer that teachers write numbers on a test? Why?
3. How did you decide how many longs, flats, and units you needed to build the numbers?
4. How did you decide which number came before and after the numbers we built?
5. How did the blocks help you understand place value?

* Reprinted with permission from *Principles and Standards for School Mathematics*, 2000 by the National Council of Teachers of Mathematics. All rights reserved.

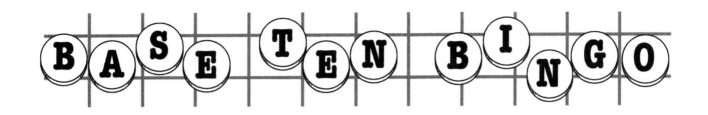

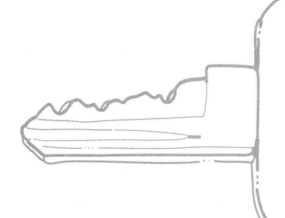

Key Question

Why is it important to recognize numbers in a variety of formats?

Learning Goals

Students will:

- build, read, and write numbers; and

- gain practice in identifying numbers written in expanded notation, as words, and as picture representations.

8 tens and 8 ones 	 70 + 8 =
An even number 	 An odd number
A number with a 5 in the ones place 	 3 tens and 9 ones
 One hundred	Thirty-one 

BASE TEN BINGO

Card A

62	31	26	49	46
16	12	22	55	88
205	53	37	28	78
35	100	65	39	42
29	235	27	98	74

AWESOME ADDITION AND SUPER SUBTRACTION © 2010 AIMS Education Foundation

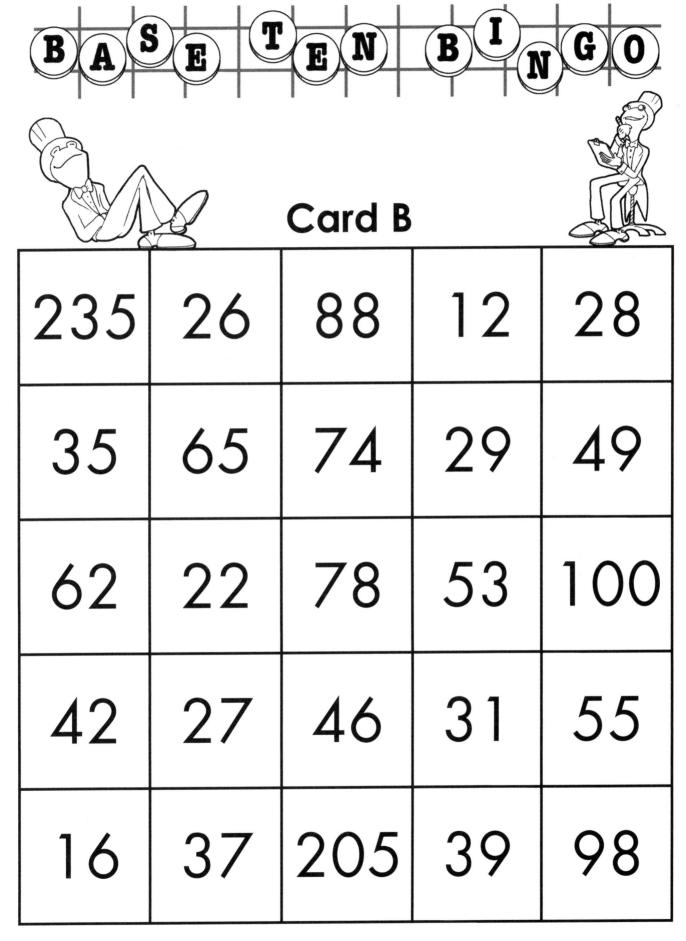

Card B

235	26	88	12	28
35	65	74	29	49
62	22	78	53	100
42	27	46	31	55
16	37	205	39	98

BASE TEN BINGO

Card C

98	27	29	235	39
42	74	46	49	26
205	100	65	31	62
88	37	53	35	22
55	12	16	78	28

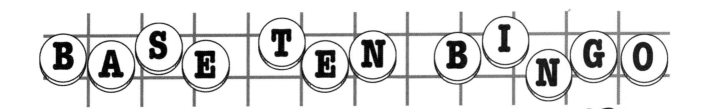

Connecting Learning

1. Which way would you prefer to write numbers? Why?

2. Which way would you prefer that teachers write numbers on a test? Why?

3. How did you decide how many longs, flats, and units you needed to build the numbers?

4. How did you decide which number came before and after the numbers we built?

5. How did the blocks help you understand place value?

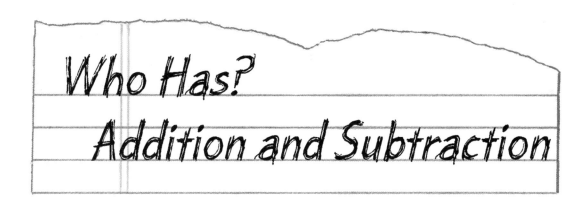

Who Has? Addition and Subtraction

Elementary students benefit from revisiting basic skills through repeated experiences in a variety of formats. While the adage *practice makes perfect* makes sense to us, there is considerable support for the idea that "drilling" for periods longer than 10 minutes a day may be counterproductive.

This learning game provides playful and intelligent practice within a very short period of time. The game features:
- an element of "playfulness,"
- minimum teacher preparation,
- time efficiency,
- mental stimulation and exercise,
- student interest and motivation, and
- 100 percent accuracy.

Management
1. Copy a set of cards on card stock.
2. Laminate the cards for durability.

Procedure
1. Distribute one card to each student or pair of students.
2. Begin the game by reading any card (for example: "I have 17. Who that number plus 2?")
3. Direct the student holding the card with the correct response (19, in the case of the example) to read his or her card ("I have 19. Who has …").
4. Continue the game until the cycle returns to the beginning card.

Who Has? Addition and Subtraction Key
1. I have 17. Who has this number plus 2?
2. I have 19. Who has this number minus 8?
3. I have 11. Who has this number minus 5?
4. I have 6. Who has this number plus 4?
5. I have 10. Who has this number plus 6?
6. I have 16. Who has this number minus 7?
7. I have 9. Who has this number minus 8?
8. I have 1. Who has this number plus 6?
9. I have 7. Who has this number plus 6?
10. I have 13. Who has this number minus 11?
11. I have 2. Who has this number plus 13?
12. I have 15. Who has this number minus 7?
13. I have 8. Who has this number minus 5?
14. I have 3. Who has this number plus 11?
15. I have 14. Who has this number minus 2?
16. I have 12. Who has this number minus 7?
17. I have 5. Who has this number plus 13?
18. I have 18. Who has this number minus 14?
19. I have 4. Who has this number minus 4?
20. I have 0. Who has this number plus 17?

AWESOME ADDITION AND SUPER SUBTRACTION

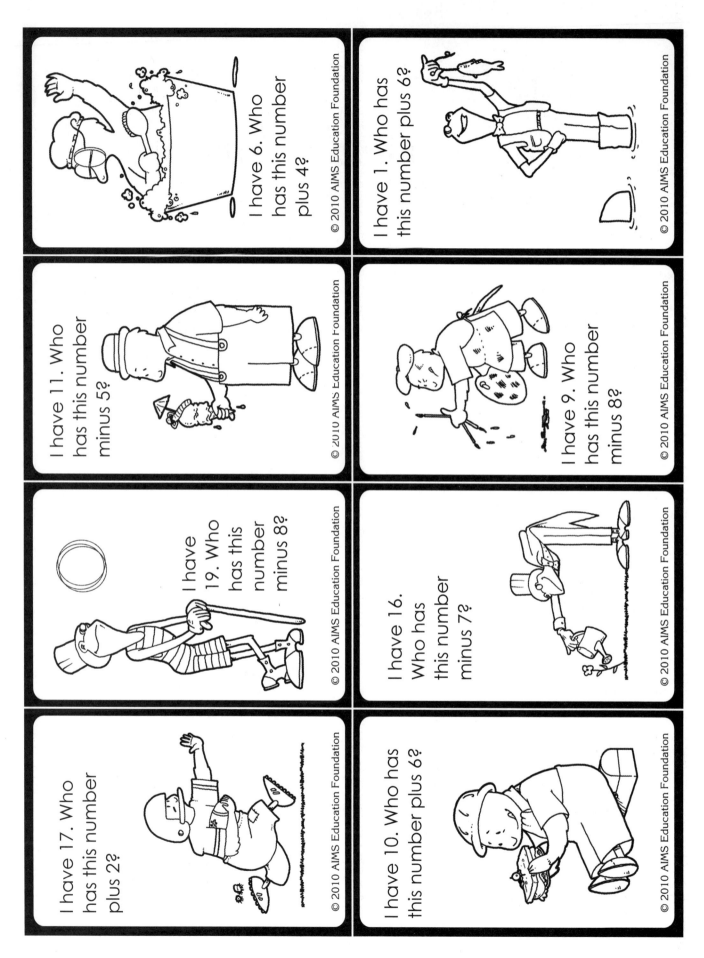

AWESOME ADDITION AND SUPER SUBTRACTION

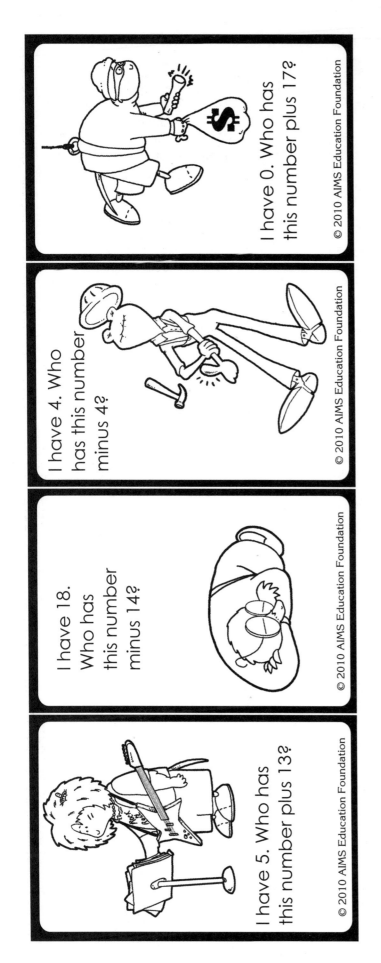

The AIMS Program

AIMS is the acronym for "**A**ctivities **I**ntegrating **M**athematics and **S**cience." Such integration enriches learning and makes it meaningful and holistic. AIMS began as a project of Fresno Pacific University to integrate the study of mathematics and science in grades K-9, but has since expanded to include language arts, social studies, and other disciplines.

AIMS is a continuing program of the non-profit AIMS Education Foundation. It had its inception in a National Science Foundation funded program whose purpose was to explore the effectiveness of integrating mathematics and science. The project directors, in cooperation with 80 elementary classroom teachers, devoted two years to a thorough field-testing of the results and implications of integration.

The approach met with such positive results that the decision was made to launch a program to create instructional materials incorporating this concept. Despite the fact that thoughtful educators have long recommended an integrative approach, very little appropriate material was available in 1981 when the project began. A series of writing projects ensued, and today the AIMS Education Foundation is committed to continuing the creation of new integrated activities on a permanent basis.

The AIMS program is funded through the sale of books, products, and professional-development workshops, and through proceeds from the Foundation's endowment. All net income from programs and products flows into a trust fund administered by the AIMS Education Foundation. Use of these funds is restricted to support of research, development, and publication of new materials. Writers donate all their rights to the Foundation to support its ongoing program. No royalties are paid to the writers.

The rationale for integration lies in the fact that science, mathematics, language arts, social studies, etc., are integrally interwoven in the real world, from which it follows that they should be similarly treated in the classroom where students are being prepared to live in that world. Teachers who use the AIMS program give enthusiastic endorsement to the effectiveness of this approach.

Science encompasses the art of questioning, investigating, hypothesizing, discovering, and communicating. Mathematics is a language that provides clarity, objectivity, and understanding. The language arts provide us with powerful tools of communication. Many of the major contemporary societal issues stem from advancements in science and must be studied in the context of the social sciences. Therefore, it is timely that all of us take seriously a more holistic method of educating our students. This goal motivates all who are associated with the AIMS Program. We invite you to join us in this effort.

Meaningful integration of knowledge is a major recommendation coming from the nation's professional science and mathematics associations. The American Association for the Advancement of Science in *Science for All Americans* strongly recommends the integration of mathematics, science, and technology. The National Council of Teachers of Mathematics places strong emphasis on applications of mathematics found in science investigations. AIMS is fully aligned with these recommendations.

Extensive field testing of AIMS investigations confirms these beneficial results:
1. Mathematics becomes more meaningful, hence more useful, when it is applied to situations that interest students.
2. The extent to which science is studied and understood is increased when mathematics and science are integrated.
3. There is improved quality of learning and retention, supporting the thesis that learning which is meaningful and relevant is more effective.
4. Motivation and involvement are increased dramatically as students investigate real-world situations and participate actively in the process.

We invite you to become part of this classroom teacher movement by using an integrated approach to learning and sharing any suggestions you may have. The AIMS Program welcomes you!

AIMS Education Foundation Programs

When you host an AIMS workshop for elementary and middle school educators, you will know your teachers are receiving effective, usable training they can apply in their classrooms immediately.

AIMS Workshops are Designed for Teachers
- Correlated to your state standards;
- Address key topic areas, including math content, science content, and process skills;
- Provide practice of activity-based teaching;
- Address classroom management issues and higher-order thinking skills;
- Give you AIMS resources; and
- Offer optional college (graduate-level) credits for many courses.

AIMS Workshops Fit District/Administrative Needs
- Flexible scheduling and grade-span options;
- Customized (one-, two-, or three-day) workshops meet specific schedule, topic, state standards, and grade-span needs;
- Prepackaged four-day workshops for in-depth math and science training available (includes all materials and expenses);
- Sustained staff development is available for which workshops can be scheduled throughout the school year;
- Eligible for funding under the Title I and Title II sections of No Child Left Behind; and
- Affordable professional development—consecutive-day workshops offer considerable savings.

University Credit—Correspondence Courses
AIMS offers correspondence courses through a partnership with Fresno Pacific University.
- Convenient distance-learning courses—you study at your own pace and schedule. No computer or Internet access required!

Introducing AIMS State-Specific Science Curriculum
Developed to meet 100% of your state's standards, AIMS' State-Specific Science Curriculum gives students the opportunity to build content knowledge, thinking skills, and fundamental science processes.
- Each grade-specific module has been developed to extend the AIMS approach to full-year science programs. Modules can be used as a complete curriculum or as a supplement to existing materials.
- Each standards-based module includes mathreading, hands-on investigations, and assessments.

Like all AIMS resources, these modules are able to serve students at all stages of readiness, making these a great value across the grades served in your school.

For current information regarding the programs described above, please complete the following form and mail it to: P.O. Box 8120, Fresno, CA 93747.

Information Request

Please send current information on the items checked:

____ *Basic Information Packet* on AIMS materials
____ Hosting information for AIMS workshops
____ AIMS State-Specific Science Curriculum

Name: _____

Phone:_____ E-mail:_____

Address: _____
        Street   City   State   Zip

YOUR K-9 MATH AND SCIENCE CLASSROOM ACTIVITIES RESOURCE

The AIMS Magazine is your source for standards-based, hands-on math and science investigations. Each issue is filled with teacher-friendly, ready-to-use activities that engage students in meaningful learning.

- *Four issues each year (fall, winter, spring, and summer).*

Current issue is shipped with all past issues within that volume.

| 1824 | Volume XXIV | 2009-2010 | $19.95 |
| 1825 | Volume XXV | 2010-2011 | $19.95 |

Two-Volume Combination

| M20810 | Volumes XXIII & XXIV | 2008-2010 | $34.95 |
| M20911 | Volumes XXIV & XXV | 2009-2011 | $34.95 |

Complete volumes available for purchase:

1802	Volume II	1987-1988	$19.95
1804	Volume IV	1989-1990	$19.95
1805	Volume V	1990-1991	$19.95
1807	Volume VII	1992-1993	$19.95
1808	Volume VIII	1993-1994	$19.95
1809	Volume IX	1994-1995	$19.95
1810	Volume X	1995-1996	$19.95
1811	Volume XI	1996-1997	$19.95
1812	Volume XII	1997-1998	$19.95
1813	Volume XIII	1998-1999	$19.95
1814	Volume XIV	1999-2000	$19.95
1815	Volume XV	2000-2001	$19.95
1816	Volume XVI	2001-2002	$19.95
1817	Volume XVII	2002-2003	$19.95
1818	Volume XVIII	2003-2004	$19.95
1819	Volume XIX	2004-2005	$19.95
1820	Volume XX	2005-2006	$19.95
1821	Volume XXI	2006-2007	$19.95
1822	Volume XXII	2007-2008	$19.95
1823	Volume XXIII	2008-2009	$19.95

Volumes II to XIX include 10 issues.

Call 1.888.733.2467 or go to www.aimsedu.org

Subscribe to the AIMS Magazine

$19.95 a year!

AIMS Magazine is published four times a year.

Subscriptions ordered at any time will receive all the issues for that year.

AIMS Online—www.aimsedu.org

To see all that AIMS has to offer, check us out on the Internet at www.aimsedu.org. At our website you can preview and purchase AIMS books and individual activities, learn about State-Specific Science and Essential Math, explore professional development workshops and online learning opportunities, search our activities database, buy manipulatives and other classroom resources, and download free resources including articles, puzzles, and sample AIMS activities.

AIMS E-mail Specials

While visiting the AIMS website, sign up for our FREE e-mail newsletter with monthly subscriber-only specials. You'll also receive advance notice of new products.

Sign up today!

AIMS Program Publications

Actions With Fractions, 4-9
The Amazing Circle, 4-9
Awesome Addition and Super Subtraction, 2-3
Bats Incredible! 2-4
Brick Layers II, 4-9
The Budding Botanist, 3-6
Chemistry Matters, 4-7
Counting on Coins, K-2
Cycles of Knowing and Growing, 1-3
Crazy About Cotton, 3-7
Critters, 2-5
Earth Book, 6-9
Electrical Connections, 4-9
Exploring Environments, K-6
Fabulous Fractions, 3-6
Fall Into Math and Science*, K-1
Field Detectives, 3-6
Finding Your Bearings, 4-9
Floaters and Sinkers, 5-9
From Head to Toe, 5-9
Glide Into Winter With Math and Science*, K-1
Gravity Rules! 5-12
Hardhatting in a Geo-World, 3-5
Historical Connections in Mathematics, Vol. I, 5-9
Historical Connections in Mathematics, Vol. II, 5-9
Historical Connections in Mathematics, Vol. III, 5-9
It's About Time, K-2
It Must Be A Bird, Pre-K-2
Jaw Breakers and Heart Thumpers, 3-5
Looking at Geometry, 6-9
Looking at Lines, 6-9
Machine Shop, 5-9
Magnificent Microworld Adventures, 6-9
Marvelous Multiplication and Dazzling Division, 4-5
Math + Science, A Solution, 5-9
Mathematicians are People, Too
Mathematicians are People, Too, Vol. II
Mostly Magnets*, 3-6
Movie Math Mania, 6-9
Multiplication the Algebra Way, 6-8
Out of This World, 4-8
Paper Square Geometry:
    The Mathematics of Origami, 5-12
Puzzle Play, 4-8
Pieces and Patterns*, 5-9

Popping With Power, 3-5
Positive vs. Negative, 6-9
Primarily Bears*, K-6
Primarily Earth, K-3
Primarily Magnets, K-2
Primarily Physics*, K-3
Primarily Plants, K-3
Primarily Weather, K-3
Problem Solving: Just for the Fun of I
Problem Solving: Just for the Fun of It! Book Two, 4-9
Proportional Reasoning, 6-9
Ray's Reflections, 4-8
Sensational Springtime, K-2
Sense-Able Science*, K-1
Shapes, Solids, and More: Concepts in Geometry, 2-3
The Sky's the Limit, 5-9
Soap Films and Bubbles, 4-9
Solve It! K-1: Problem-Solving Strategies, K-1
Solve It! 2nd: Problem-Solving Strategies, 2
Solve It! 3rd: Problem-Solving Strategies, 3
Solve It! 4th: Problem-Solving Strategies, 4
Solve It! 5th: Problem-Solving Strategies, 5
Solving Equations: A Conceptual Approach, 6-9
Spatial Visualization, 4-9
Spills and Ripples, 5-12
Spring Into Math and Science*, K-1
Statistics and Probability, 6-9
Through the Eyes of the Explorers, 5-9
Under Construction, K-2
Water, Precious Water, 4-6
Weather Sense: Temperature, Air Pressure, and Wind, 4-5
Weather Sense: Moisture, 4-5
What's Next, Volume 1, 4-12
What's Next, Volume 2, 4-12
What's Next, Volume 3, 4-12
Winter Wonders, K-2

Essential Math
Area Formulas for Parallelograms, Triangles, and Trapazoids, 6-8
Measurement of Prisms, Pyramids, Cylinders, and Cones, 6-8
Circumference and Area of Circles, 5-7
Measurement of Rectangular Solids, 5-7
The Pythagorean Relationship, 6-8

Spanish Edition
Constructores II: Ingeniería Creativa Con Construcciones
    LEGO®, 4-9
    The entire book is written in Spanish. English pages not included.

* Spanish supplements are available for these books. They are only available as downloads from the AIMS website. The supplements contain only the student pages in Spanish; you will need the English version of the book for the teacher's text.

For further information, contact:
AIMS Education Foundation • P.O. Box 8120 • Fresno, California 93747-8120
www.aimsedu.org • 559.255.6396 (fax) • 888.733.2467 (toll free)

Duplication Rights

No part of any AIMS books, magazines, activities, or content—digital or otherwise—may be reproduced or transmitted in any form or by any means—including photocopying, taping, or information storage/retrieval systems—except as noted below.

Standard Duplication Rights

- A person or school purchasing AIMS activities (in books, magazines, or in digital form) is hereby granted permission to make up to 200 copies of any portion of those activities, provided these copies will be used for educational purposes and only at one school site.
- Workshop or conference presenters may make one copy of any portion of a purchased activity for each participant, with a limit of five activities per workshop or conference session.
- All copies must bear the AIMS Education Foundation copyright information.

Standard duplication rights apply to activities received at workshops, free sample activities provided by AIMS, and activities received by conference participants.

Unlimited Duplication Rights

Unlimited duplication rights may be purchased in cases where AIMS users wish to:
- make more than 200 copies of a book/magazine/activity,
- use a book/magazine/activity at more than one school site, or
- make an activity available on the Internet (see below).

These rights permit unlimited duplication of purchased books, magazines, and/or activities (including revisions) for use at a given school site.

Activities received at workshops are eligible for upgrade from standard to unlimited duplication rights.

Free sample activities and activities received as a conference participant are not eligible for upgrade from standard to unlimited duplication rights.

State-Specific Science modules are licensed to one classroom/one teacher and are therefore not eligible for upgrade from standard to unlimited duplication rights.

Upgrade Fees

The fees for upgrading from standard to unlimited duplication rights are:
- $5 per activity per site,
- $25 per book per site, and
- $10 per magazine issue per site.

The cost of upgrading is shown in the following examples:
- activity: 5 activities x 5 sites x $5 = $125
- book: 10 books x 5 sites x $25 = $1250
- magazine issue: 1 issue x 5 sites x $10 = $50

Purchasing Unlimited Duplication Rights

To purchase unlimited duplication rights, please provide us the following:
1. The name of the individual responsible for coordinating the purchase of duplication rights.
2. The title of each book, activity, and magazine issue to be covered.
3. The number of school sites and name of each site for which rights are being purchased.
4. Payment (check, purchase order, credit card)

Requested duplication rights are automatically authorized with payment. The individual responsible for coordinating the purchase of duplication rights will be sent a certificate verifying the purchase.

Internet Use

AIMS materials may be made available on the Internet if all of the following stipulations are met:
1. The materials to be put online are purchased as PDF files from AIMS (i.e., no scanned copies).
2. Unlimited duplication rights are purchased for all materials to be put online for each school at which they will be used. (See above.)
3. The materials are made available via a secure, password-protected system that can only be accessed by employees at schools for which duplication rights have been purchased.

AIMS materials may not be made available on any publicly accessible Internet site.